BITCOIN
EVERYTHING YOU NEED TO KNOW

DAVID ST-ONGE

translated by
Henry J.K.I. Young * Jonathan LeBlanc

BITCOIN
EVERYTHING YOU NEED TO KNOW

OTHER BOOKS BY THIS AUTHOR

Tout sur Bitcoin : le comprendre et l'utiliser, Dicoland, 2021

OTHER BOOKS IN THE SAME COLLECTION

MOUGAYAR William, *Business blockchain : pratiques et applications professionnelles*, 2017

ANTONOPOULOS Andreas, *L'Internet de l'argent, volume 1, Recueil de conférences*, 2018

AMMOUS Saifedean, *L'Étalon-Bitcoin : l'alternative décentralisée aux banques centrales*, 2019

DE FILIPPI Primavera, *Blockchain & Droit, le règne du code*, 2019

PRITZKER Yan, *L'Invention de Bitcoin : la technologie expliquée de A à Z*, 2020

BHATIA Nik, *La Monnaie pyramide : de l'or, au dollar, au Bitcoin et aux monnaies numériques des banques centrales*, 2022

Copyright @2023, Dicoland
98, Bd du Montparnasse
75014 Paris
https://www.dicoland.com
Legal deposit : March 2023
Item number 37486121
ISBN 9782856083857

TABLE OF CONTENTS

TABLE OF CONTENTS

TABLE OF CONTENTS

FOREWORD

Year after year, Bitcoin is becoming more and more mainstream. Gone are the days where someone would ask me, "What is Bitcoin?" Everybody has heard about it, even though for the vast majority, their knowledge is very superficial. But on the road towards mass adoption—which we are still far away from—this book by David St-Onge is clearly needed to help your friends, family, and anyone else gain a good understanding of what Bitcoin is, beyond the 10 second clips offered by the mainstream media.

In this book, David covers the foundation of money, its origins, as well as some important historical hyperinflationary events with government-run currencies. After all, when governments are in trouble, and with elections always around the corner, it is much easier to blame outside factors such as "supply chains" than to face the hard facts about the financial crisis.

If you ask anyone on the street how government money or central banks work, they will have no clue. And for those in the know, they all realize that the central bank's decisions on interest rates are arbitrary and have huge effects on everyone's life.

Bitcoin's code is open source. Its protocol, its corresponding blockchain, and all the activities on it are visible to anyone at any time. This means that no such arbitrary decisions can be made for you. David explains the core elements needed for the man on the street to grasp this important fact.

You might have heard a few words here and there about Bitcoin that might have scared you, but rest assured: after reading "Bitcoin: Everything you need to know," you will have demystified terms such as "hash,"

"SHA256," "UTXOs," how to manage a Bitcoin wallet and its relation with Bitcoin addresses, and many more such core topics, including the most important one of all—how to send and receive bitcoins.

People need to realize how important it is to be custodians of their own wallets. Bitcoin does not need a bank or any other third party, and yet, too many are leaving their bitcoin on exchanges. With the recent FTX debacle, we have seen that exchanges are never the safest places to store your coins. "Bank bailouts" are not possible with Bitcoin as it cannot be inflated at will in order to socialize the losses; this virtue comes with the necessity for each and every one of us to be more responsible, and that's where this book can help you remove any fear towards this important goal!

Enjoy reading this fantastic book by my friend David!

Phil Champagne

PREFACE

"Writing a description for this thing for general audiences is bloody hard. There's nothing to relate it to."

—Satoshi Nakamoto

The idea to write this book came to me during a dinner party with my friends. I had just given one of them the course notes I had prepared for my students. At one point, she stopped reading, looked at me, and asked: "Why don't you write a book?" To which I spontaneously answered: "But I can't write a book if I have nothing to say!" I had written hundreds of pages of lecture notes, collated from several reference books on the subject, and I had listed and structured many interesting and/or relevant observations gathered from here and there, but practically none of the words were my own. How could I possibly turn it into a book? Did I have anything interesting to add on this fascinating subject?

After I started giving the course, I quickly realized that these notes didn't answer every question. Prompted by my students, I added precisions, refined explanations, and opened countless parentheses... Clearly, I had a lot to say on the subject! Hence the goal of this book: to lay out the usefulness as well as the nuts and bolts of Bitcoin as clearly and simply as possible, accompanied by anecdotes from Twitter and Medium, but also personal experiences of my own.

This book aims for a wide audience, going all the way down the rabbit hole while also remaining accessible to the layman. My hope is that by the time you reach the end of this book, you will have a good understanding of Bitcoin without slipping into hyper-technicalities. You will have all the tools you need to wrap your head around how Bitcoin works and, above all, the political philosophy that led to its creation (yes, Bitcoin is a political act).

To understand Bitcoin, you also need to understand the blockchain, the technology which Bitcoin is built upon, which brings us notably to the concept of Proof-of-Work (PoW). For those of you who are curious about this and other trickier subjects, suggestions for extra reading material will be given throughout the book, handpicked either for their educational value, or simply because it's a must-read on the subject.

The purpose of this book is to demystify the subject of Bitcoin, and should not be construed as an incentive to invest in it. My publisher and I are convinced that sharing this knowledge is essential now that Bitcoin has firmly established itself in the financial landscape, despite the savage onslaught by "orthodox" skeptics, and anyone else that fears that Bitcoin will deprive them of the absolute power conferred to them by centralized state-issued currencies.

David St-Onge

INTRODUCTION

"If enough people think the same way, that becomes a self fulfilling prophecy."

—SATOSHI NAKAMOTO

Bitcoin is terrible at making a good first impression. Generally, one has to be properly introduced to it before being able to give it the attention it deserves. The first time I heard about it, I was left with the impression that it was just another techno gadget for next-level geeks who enjoy collecting virtual tokens on the Internet. I thought that these geeks were hellbent on tricking "normies" into believing that these tokens could be worth something one day. But how can something have any value if it can't even be seen or touched?

That was the extent of my interest for a while until a colleague initiated me to the concept of mining cryptocurrencies. Seeing him mine a non-Bitcoin cryptocurrency (Monero) with leftover computer parts piqued my curiosity. I was warming up to the idea of blockchains, but only for the novelty of it. At that point, I had no idea how they actually worked. Much like you can drive a car without understanding the inner workings of a combustion engine or manual transmission... until you're stranded on the highway, clueless, with smoke oozing out of the engine block. Even though I didn't really understand it, I ventured into "altcoin"[1] mining for a while. Then, I discovered Bitcoin.

---

1   "Altcoin" is a term used to describe all cryptocurrencies other than Bitcoin.

Influenced by information circulating in traditional media, my initial belief was that Bitcoin was only used by criminals. Why in the world would any "normal" person use a virtual currency? I preferred getting paid in dollars, directly deposited into my account, at the same bank in which I had been depositing my savings since teenagehood.

Seemingly proving me right, after seeing an all-time high of 20,000 USD[2] at one point, Bitcoin quickly crashed into oblivion. My feed was filled with a daily barrage of "obituary" editorials, all heralding the imminent end of Bitcoin. Meanwhile, a group of high-level geeks, like veterans trying to rally new recruits on the battlefield, were writing books, posting tweets, and producing a host of podcasts in an effort to filter out all the "noise," empower people, and help them decipher Bitcoin.

These first-generation bitcoiners had already seen their fair share of volatility in the coin's first decade. While spectacular, the last unstoppable rise and cataclysmic fall of Bitcoin wasn't the first bubble they had powered through. If anything, this book is a homage to those pioneers. Without them, I would never have understood how Bitcoin works, not to mention how much it has changed the way I relate to money and to the free market principles that made money useful in the first place.

This book provides a quick overview of the motivations that led to Bitcoin's inception and explains why Bitcoin is relevant. It draws a parallel between the characteristics of Bitcoin's protocol on the one side, and the problems inherent to state-issued currencies on the other (Part I). Then, we delve into how to use it. Too much is said and written about Bitcoin without explaining this piece of the puzzle, which we will address in Part II of the book. Thirdly, we will break down the main obstacles to Bitcoin adoption (Chapter 8), and reflect on Bitcoin's future (Chapter 9). Last but not least, we will share the transcripts of interviews that I conducted with actual bitcoiners, so that their personal experience can help those of you who are just getting started on this journey.

I had to read a lot of books to wrap my head around Bitcoin. Many were never meant to be used for educational purposes. Some are downright unreadable, a tangled mess of technical gibberish that elicits nothing but frustration and profanity. To bring back our car example from earlier, the

---

2   Bitcoin's price surpassed 69,000 USD in November 2021 before falling below 20,000 USD in 2022.

sort of book that goes into exhaustive detail about the inner workings of a manual transmission box, without ever explaining why it's important in the first place. *Bitcoin: Everything You Need to Know* is my answer to that: it not only gives readers a solid grasp of the fundamentals, but most importantly, a place to start.

Part I
BITCOIN EXPLAINED

CHAPTER 1.
BITCOIN IS GOOD MONEY

"I've been working on a new electronic cash system that's fully peer-to-peer, with no trusted third party."

—SATOSHI NAKAMOTO

To understand why Bitcoin was born, let's look at the considerations that guided its inventor. To elucidate this matter, we will explore his writings regarding the Global Financial Crisis, as well as the characteristics that constitute a good form of money.

THE MOTIVATIONS BEHIND BITCOIN

As stated in the preface, Bitcoin's invention is a political act. The individual or group of people[3] that invented Bitcoin, known only by the alias of Satoshi Nakamoto, never shied away from this fact. It isn't a coincidence that Bitcoin was launched right after the Global Financial Crisis. If we pay attention to Satoshi Nakamoto's writings, it becomes glaringly obvious that

---

3   Read the interview with Francis Pouliot at the end of the book, in which he tells me that he is convinced that Bitcoin was created by a specific group of cypherpunks. According to him, Satoshi Nakamoto is probably one of these individuals, or perhaps a name representing the entire group. Francis also suggests that Satoshi's identity may not have been known to the members of this group.

providing an alternative to fiat currencies[4] and breaking state monopolies to restore individual sovereignty were the main motivations behind Bitcoin's creation. In November 2008, addressed by a user on a forum board regarding the impossibility to resolve political problems through the use of cryptography, Satoshi answered with the following:

"Governments are good at cutting off the heads of a centrally controlled networks like Napster, but pure P2P networks like Gnutella and Tor seem to be holding their own."

Satoshi also clearly states that his new system is designed to allow individuals to bypass banks. In February 2009, he writes the following on p2pfoundation.ning.com :

"Banks must be trusted to hold our money and transfer it electronically, but they lend it out in waves of credit bubbles with barely a fraction in reserve."

Bitcoin aims to offer the world an alternative to the current financial system, the very system that was responsible for the 2008 crisis. Thanks to a mechanism that limits the emission of new bitcoins—which we will cover later—Bitcoin is the remedy to central banks inflating the monetary supply. As we will see, scarcity is one of the key criteria when looking for good money.

WHAT IS GOOD MONEY?

In the first part of his seminal book, *The Bitcoin Standard,*[5] economist Saifedean Ammous gives us a history class on the evolution of money and financial systems. We'll give you an overview of the essentials here, but you can refer to *The Bitcoin Standard* for further reading if you find yourself particularly interested in the content of this chapter.

Ammous defines money as such:

> *"Any person choosing to purchase something not for its own sake, but with the aim of exchanging it for something else, is*

---

4   Fiat money is a type of currency whose face value (the value on the bill) is guaranteed by an institution, such as a government, not by a commodity such as gold or silver.

5   Saifedean Ammous, *The Bitcoin Standard*, 2018.

*making it de facto money, and as people vary, so do their opin-
ions on, and choices of, what constitutes money."*

He thus deconstructs the widely held belief that money is exclusively under the authority of a state. What really interests him, however, is
defining what good money is, because only a good form of money can
guarantee the enrichment of its holders, as well as the development of
investment and art. According to him, good money allows society to share
a common unit of account, fostering investments and serving as a store
of value for the holder. For this to happen, it needs to be durable (coincidence of time), easily transportable (coincidence of space), easily divided
into smaller units (coincidence of scales), and especially hard to (re)pro-
duce.

MULTIPLE COINCIDENCES

To explore the concepts of coincidence of time, space and scales, let's
refer to a very interesting book by Michael Caras, *Bitcoin Money: A Tale
of Bitville Discovering Good Money.*[6] The author tells the tale of a small
town and its young inhabitants, who discover together, through trial and
error, what makes good money. The book illustrates how the townsfolk
attempt to exchange goods and services between each other. For instance,
one child offers another child to mow his lawn in exchange for five glasses
of frozen lemonade. The next day, disappointed that the lemonades are
no longer cold, the child offers to mow the lawn again in exchange for
more frozen lemonade. But obviously, a lawn doesn't need to be mowed
every day. This example shows a lack of coincidence of time, as one of
the children wishes to acquire a good that is not needed by his friend at
that moment in time. And if he instead offered a bicycle in exchange for
the lemonade, he would then be confronted with a lack of coincidence of
scales. Realistically, you won't find someone with a lemonade stock that's
worth as much as a bike. And even if you were to find someone with that
much lemonade, it wouldn't stay fresh for very long. Once again, we find
ourselves with no coincidence of time.

As for the coincidence of space, we might picture a child who wants
to trade his hazelnut tree in exchange for his neighbor's apple tree. Even
if the two trees had equal value and the neighbor agreed to go through

---

6   Michael Caras, *Bitcoin Money: A Tale of Bitville Discovering Good Money*, 2019.

with the trade, transplanting two large trees is far beyond the means of a couple of small children!

Keeping in mind these four factors that constitute good money, let's consider gold, which has an almost-perfect score on three of these attributes. Gold's chemical stability renders it nearly indestructible (coincidence of time). All the gold that has ever been extracted from the Earth since the dawn of time still exists on the surface today, having kept its value over the millennia. Gold is therefore durable, both physically and economically. Gold is also relatively easy to transport. A few ounces represent great value, so we can move large sums in gold without occupying too much space (coincidence of space). Gold also has the distinctive feature of being naturally scarce. Considerable efforts are required to extract it from the Earth's crust, which ensures its scarcity. However, when it comes to divisibility (coincidence of scales), gold does not fare particularly well. Paying someone in grams of gold just isn't very practical: you have to scrape little pieces off before putting them on a scale. During the centuries in which gold was used as money, silver was the perfect solution to this particular problem. Silver coins were used for smaller transactions, giving birth to the bimetallic system that solved gold's problem pertaining to coincidences of scales.

With the advent of banks, banknotes that were redeemable in gold made it divisible on every scale, ushering in the end of silver's use as money.

STOCK-TO-FLOW RATIO

In *The Bitcoin Standard*, Ammous introduces us to the concept of the stock-to-flow ratio, which is the relationship between a good's existing stock and the additional production of that good over a given timeframe. A high stock-to-flow ratio indicates that the production of a good in a given period is low compared to the existing stock. Gold is the ultimate example of a good that has a high stock-to-flow ratio. As we already know, all the gold that has ever been extracted still exists today. The gold that gets produced does not get consumed (in contrast to most commodities). Consequently, the yearly production of gold will never be higher than a very small percentage of the existing stock. For a good to be used as money, it needs to be relatively scarce.

That isn't to say that scarcity goes through the roof when the stock runs out. It is the difficulty of obtaining a good that makes it scarce. If gold weren't as hard as it is to extract, we would be producing much more of it, and the stock-to-flow ratio would thus suffer. But even if we were to double the production rate, the stock-to-flow ratio would remain high. The same cannot be said for almost all other goods on the market. In the words of Ammous:

> *"To understand the difference between gold and any consumable commodity, imagine the effect of a large increase in demand for it as a store of value that causes the price to spike and annual production to double. For any consumable commodity, this doubling of output will dwarf any existing stockpiles, bringing the price crashing down and hurting the holders. For gold, a price spike that causes a doubling of annual production will be insignificant, increasing stockpiles by 3% rather than 1.5%. If the new increased pace of production is maintained, the stockpiles grow faster, making new increases less significant. It remains practically impossible for goldminers to mine quantities of gold large enough to depress the price significantly."*

THE ROLES OF MONEY

Now that we understand what makes good money, let's dive into its functions. Since the dawn of civilization, money has been primarily used as a medium of exchange. Which brings us to another passage from *The Bitcoin Standard* by Saifedean Ammous:

> *"Being a medium of exchange is the quintessential function that defines money—in other words, it is a good purchased not to be consumed [...], but primarily for the sake of being exchanged for other goods."*

A good becomes money when it is acquired not so that it can be used for its own properties, but to be exchanged for another good.

Once a good becomes well established and widely used as a medium of exchange, it can become a unit of account, serving as a "measure" that tells us the value of things. Take the example of a primitive fisherman living on an island, fishing almost exclusively for his sustenance. He has to fish every day, day after day, just to ensure his survival. What's worse, even on a good day, he can't accumulate stocks of fish because fish doesn't stay fresh for very long. But one day, the inhabitant of a neighboring island offers some salt in exchange for a few fish. Using this newly acquired salt to preserve some of his fish, the fisherman is now able to accumulate a certain quantity of extra food to ensure his survival. He can now take a few days off to build a raft, which makes his fishing even more efficient. More and more fish are hauled out of the ocean, to the point that he's now able to feed the entire town. At that point, fish and salt have become the currency of our fictional little village. In our example, the value of goods and services could be calculated in pounds of salt or salted fish, which goes a long way to facilitate commercial exchanges. Hence the third role of money: to allow some sort of standardization when calculating the value of goods by serving as a unit of account.

Last but not least, another essential role of money is to store value. Good money with high durability across time, chemically as well as economically, allows individuals to store their savings… as long as it's scarce, i.e. hard to reproduce.

CHAPTER 2.
MONETARY HAZARDS

"The Times 03/Jan/2009 Chancellor on brink of second bailout for banks."

-Genesis block's secret message

Money hasn't always been a state monopoly. In fact, when looking at human history in its entirety, the current monopoly is very recent. For centuries, people were able to choose the best money for themselves, and when it was a good one, society profited from increased economic growth as well as all the advantages that come out of such growth. In contrast, as we'll see in this chapter, many states have failed monumentally in their currency management, with heavy consequences for their populations: devaluation or inflation, and in extreme cases, hyperinflation.

INFLATION

Inflation is a phenomenon whereby the prices of goods and services increase. This increase can simply be the result of more demand and/or less availability for that good or service. It is a natural phenomenon tied to the principle of supply and demand. However, inflation—the general increase of prices—can also be defined as a loss in the purchasing power of a given currency.

Nowadays, inflation is literally "remote-controlled" by central banks. Central banks all have an inflation target, which they attempt to reach through the use of their tools of choice, such as the key interest rates at which they lend liquidities to the country's banks, as well as the quantity of money that they issue. By adjusting the key interest rate, a central bank exerts indirect control over the country's Gross Domestic Product. A weak key interest rate exacerbates the volume of loans, as banks will seize the opportunity of cheap credit from their central bank to in turn issue more loans. The same phenomenon occurs when a central bank increases the quantity of money in circulation. The influx of capital usually results in a higher GDP, which indirectly influences the inflation rate. A central bank will continually adjust its monetary policy to reach the inflation target. For instance, that target is currently 2% at the Bank of Canada.[7]

Inflation encourages spending and therefore consumerism. Better to spend that money now, because it'll be worth less tomorrow. During periods of extreme inflation, called hyperinflation, there can be different prices for a given good depending on the type of payment you use to purchase it. For example, there could be one price for cash payments and another for cheques, because depositing a cheque into your account can take several days, and the price might just double in that time, cutting the actual value of the payment in half. In the Western world, we are used to modest inflation rates and will rarely be confronted with this kind of situation. But the effects are still there, albeit more subtle.

DEVALUATION IN THE ERA OF FIAT MONEY

This "programmed" inflation is not a recent development. Although the financial system of Ancient Rome was based on actual metal coins, this didn't stop certain emperors from devaluing their currency by reducing the amount of precious metals held in these coins. Even if modern coins are no longer exchanged for the value of the metals they're made of, and are instead traded for their face value, they are still not immune to this subterfuge. When I go to the park with my kids, I often see the glimmer of coins lying on the ground. I developed a habit of picking them up and "cold-storing" them in the corner of my balcony. I noticed that some of these coins fared better than others in Quebec's harsh winters. Two

7   https://www.bankofcanada.ca/core-functions/monetary-policy

nickels stood out in particular, one of them made in 1979 and the other in 2016. Exposed to the elements, the 1979 coin was simply tarnished, while the 2016 coin was corroded. Intrigued, I looked it up on the website of the Royal Canadian Mint and found out that the 1979 one was made of 99.9% nickel, while the 2016 one was 94.5% steel with a thin coat of nickel.

1979 and 2016 Canadian nicels (author's personal collection).

This change in the makeup of the coin can be explained by the constant inflation pushed by central banks. As they devalue the currency, the metal making up the coins ends up being worth more than the nominal value, at which point the Mint has no other choice but to fall back on cheaper materials like steel. In Canada, pennies were once minted with copper, then with steel, before being outright discontinued. Which material will they use once the value of steel surpasses the nominal value of the coins that are made out of it? Plastic? Your guess is as good as mine.

A one ruble plastic coin from Transnistria - 2014 (author's personal collection).

HYPERINFLATION: HISTORY REPEATS ITSELF

The problems related to liquidity and funding have marked history in multiple instances. One of the best-known cases of hyperinflation was the Weimar Republic after World War I, where the turmoil culminated in a whopping 29,500% yearly inflation rate, which translates to 20.9% per day. Prices doubled every 3.7 days![8] The story goes that restaurant owners had to change the prices on their menus every 30 minutes to keep up. It is said that a client once ordered 2 coffees at 5,000 Marks each, only to find that he had to pay 14,000 Marks by the time he had finished drinking his second cup of coffee.[9]

The state that experienced the worst hyperinflation in history is no doubt Hungary after World War II. They found themselves on the losing side of the conflict, which had wiped out its industrial production capacity. In 1946, the yearly inflation rate went up to $4,19*10^{16}$%, equivalent to 207% per day. Prices doubled every 15 hours![10]

THE CASE OF ZIMBABWE

Up until 2000, Zimbabwe was almost completely self-sufficient, except when it came to petroleum. In 1999, it had a positive trade balance, i.e. it was a net exporter in agriculture, but became a net importer by 2003. In February 2000, after the population rejected a referendum on the "redistribution program" of agricultural land, veterans of the War of Independence began seizing land from owners of European descent with the government's approval. This caused a massive capital flight, in turn causing a shortage of currency within the country's borders and a thriving black market. In November 2003, you needed 6,000 ZWD to buy 1 USD on the black market, while the official rate was only 824 ZWD. Of course, the price of goods and services did not reflect the official government rate but that of the black market, which even legitimate businesses started using eventually.

In addition to the shortage of foreign currencies, the continual increase

---

8   https://www.cato.org/research/world-inflation-and-hyperinflation-table

9   https://www.mentalfloss.com/article/518399/hyperinflation-gone-mad-when-german-children- made-kites-money

10   https://www.cato.org/research/world-inflation-and-hyperinflation-table

in prices caused a shortage of local banknotes. The more prices went up, the more people needed additional banknotes to buy their goods. For example, an item which had previously cost a single 20 ZWD bill a month ago would now cost 40 ZWD. Hence a vicious circle: the more prices go up, the more banknotes are needed, and the more banknotes are thus printed out to meet the demand, resulting in inflation. Faced with this steady increase in prices, salaries that were usually adjusted yearly had to be adjusted monthly, then every payday. In 2001, the state demanded that 40% of export income be handed over to the Central Bank. In September 2003, bearer checks were introduced in order to offer higher denominations and ease the currency demand. In December, inflation reached 455%. The Central Bank of Zimbabwe took control of currency exchanges and set up auctions for distribution. In 2005, inflation reached 586%, followed by a 50% monthly rate in March 2007. Some managers were forced to hire workers simply to count the astronomical volume of banknotes piling up in their vaults. In June 2007, the government reacted by instating price controls. Stores were literally raided and left empty as these government prices were too low, making the owners unable to resupply. Soon, the population was confronted with withdrawal limits at the bank. Only 5 million ZWN per person per day, for instance—a loaf of bread was worth as high as 2 million ZWN. In his book *Hard-Boiled Egg Index: Surviving Zimbabwe's Hyperinflation*, Kudzai Joseph Gumunyu recounts that one morning, a client at his bank called, claiming he was expecting to see a 1.5 trillion ZWN balance in his account, only to find a mere 150 billion. Because the bank's computer system could not display numbers higher than 999 billion, they had decided to divide the value of all bank accounts by 1,000 and multiply the value by 1,000 upon withdrawal.[11] In 2009, the Central Bank of Zimbabwe removed 12 zeroes from its currency and introduced 7 new banknotes in an attempt to inject more physical bills into the economy.

In his book *Zimbabwe: Warm Heart Ugly Face*, Jerome Gardner describes the impact of this removal of 12 zeroes on the price of a skirt: "This skirt, which used to be worth 520 ZWR on August 13 (5.2 trillion ZWN before removing the zeroes), was sold at 21,600 ZWR on September 8. On September 11, three days later, the same skirt went for 43,200 ZWR! The following week, the price climbed to 86,400 ZWR, and on October 2, i.e. a mere two weeks later, it was already at 1,728,000 ZWR. On October

---

11 Kudzai Joseph Gumunyu, *Hard-Boiled Egg Index: Surviving Zimbabwe's Hyperinflation*, 2019.

20, 2008, our skirt was worth 414 million ZWR."[12] Thus, in the space of a few weeks, the selling price had already recovered 6 of the 12 zeroes that had just been slashed! The situation reached a point where people preferred using fuel coupons as money. Since a coupon for 20L was still worth 20L the next day, the next week, and even the next month, it was a far better store of value than the Zimbabwean dollar. Not to mention the fact that gas suppliers actually ensured that they had enough gas in stock to honor the coupons they were issuing, which cannot be said of our central banks!

The exponential explosion of inflation rates was probably fuelled even further by the "anticipated" inflation that affected business owners who had lost all faith in the local currency. Many suppliers were forced to become less flexible with their payment terms and started adjusting their prices in anticipation of inflation. For example, if a retail store chain ordered shoes at 1 USD a pair—equivalent to 10 billion Zimbabwean dollars—and wanted to pay the invoice 30 days later, the supplier anticipated the inflation and charged them 70 billion per pair of shoes. The consumer was then forced to pay 120 billion instead of the 18 billion it would've cost them if the business had paid the supplier upfront. This "anticipated" inflation only further contributed to the inflationary spiral.

Then there is the concept of "burner prices." With all these variations in the inflation and exchange rates, some "entrepreneurs" saw the opportunity to make profits. In his aforementioned book, Jerome Gardner explains the strategy: an entrepreneur sells 10 USD for a balance of Zimbabwean dollars at a very advantageous rate. Next, he uses that balance to pay for 10 pairs of trousers by cheque. He then sells the trousers at a 30% or even 50% discount to ensure a quick sale, but only for USD or South African Rands, at which point he repeats the same formula, this time buying 30 pairs of trousers at a profit. In economic terms, this operation is called arbitrage. Businesses realized the extent of this practice and immediately raised prices to prevent it, contributing once again even more to the inflation spiral. In the end, many merchants simply stopped taking cheques. For some, this effectively meant cutting off sales entirely since the cash withdrawal limits at the bank were so strict.

On January 16, 2009, the central bank launched the infamous "trillion" dollar notes. That was the straw that broke the camel's back. According to

---

12 Jerome Gardner, *Zimbabwe: Warm Heart Ugly Face*, 2010

the author Kudzai Joseph Gumunyu mentioned earlier, it was at that moment that people stopped using Zimbabwean banknotes. In April 2009, the minister of finance announced that they were suspending the Zimbabwean dollar, and authorized the use of different foreign currencies (US dollar, British pound, euro, rand, pula). All bank accounts, pensions, and financial institutions saw their balances vanish overnight. No one was spared. The entire population and every institution had to start from scratch.

In conclusion, here are a few more examples gleaned from my readings about the devastating effects of hyperinflation. Concerning the extreme precarity this brings onto businesses, whose services are paid for weeks or even months after goods or services are charged—like energy suppliers, for example—Kudzai Joseph tells us: "If someone owed you money, a day felt like an eternity because of hyperinflation. A power bill due in two months? Let's just say it was worth nothing upon payment. In most cases, the money had lost over 80% of its value in the meantime." The author describes a situation where during power outages, for lack of means, equipment and fuel, consumers had to go and fetch technicians using their own vehicles to get the power back on. As if that wasn't enough, people went as far as taking the copper out of the electrical equipment to sell it, or the oil from the transformers to use in their car engines.[13] To protect themselves against the devaluation of their currency, taxi drivers charged higher on the way back, and made sure to trade in their local currency for foreign banknotes multiple times a day.[14]

DEFLATION

On the other side of the spectrum, deflation is defined as the decrease in the price of goods and services. In a deflationary society, a dollar earned today will be worth more tomorrow. Given that modern economies are literally fueled by debt and credit issued by banks, it isn't desirable for a bank to see your house be worth less than the mortgage they gave you. This is in part why central banks not only limit inflation on the upside

13 Kudzai Joseph Gumunyu, *Hard-Boiled Egg Index: Surviving Zimbabwe's Hyperinflation*, op. cit.

14 https://webcache.googleusercontent.com/search?q=cache:s3k76JBtR-EJ:https://www.economist.com/middle-east-and-africa/2008/07/17/a-worthless-currency+&cd=3&hl=en&ct=clnk&gl=ca

at around 2 or 3%, but also limit it at a floor of about 1%. What we have here is an "inflation-control target, which is 2%, the midpoint of a 1 to 3% target range."[15] Yet deflation actually sounds like a good thing (and it is, at least in my humble opinion). Wouldn't it be wonderful if every dollar you earned meant more and more purchasing power over time?

However, there are dark clouds looming on the horizon for the central banks' inflation-deflation parade. In *The Price of Tomorrow*, Jeff Booth puts forth the idea that technological innovation and the exponential growth of technology (automation, cheap renewable energy, and the rise of AI for example) are setting the stage for an inexorable deflationary future. The author also points out that even the tools used by central banks have limits, and won't be able to contain the deflationary effects of innovation indefinitely. This does not sound reassuring for the banks and their mortgages.

BITCOIN FIXES THIS

In December 2009, on the BitcoinTalk forum, Satoshi wrote the following regarding coins that could potentially be lost forever:

> *"Those coins can never be recovered, and the total circulation is less. Since the effective circulation is reduced, all the remaining coins are worth slightly more. It's the opposite of when a government prints money and the value of existing money goes down."*

Satoshi hints at the role of central banks in devaluing money. He highlights the fact that the sum of lost bitcoins will have a deflationary effect on all the other coins in circulation. Which is why Satoshi included enough decimal places in the Bitcoin protocol to support Bitcoin's inevitable, natural deflation, and perhaps even the deflationary future of the economy. Each bitcoin can be subdivided into 100,000,000 units. This unit is called a *satoshi*, after its creator. Here's what he had to say on this subject on bitcointalk.org back in February 2010:

> *"If there's massive deflation in the future, the software could show more decimal places."*

---

15 https://www.bankofcanada.ca/core-functions/monetary-policy

But moving beyond the deflationary effect of lost bitcoins, the fixed number of bitcoins is Nakamoto's solution to limit the monetary supply. There will never be more than 21 million bitcoins. We'll soon see how this is possible.

As for central banks, they will always find an urgent, pressing reason to increase the volume of the monetary supply. History teaches this to us time and time again. Today, we don't need to look any further than the sanitary crisis of COVID-19 for a prime example.

But Bitcoin's monetary policy is immutable. Nothing can ever change it. Nothing could increase the number of available bitcoins beyond the protocol's limit. That is why Bitcoin's monetary policy is beyond a shadow of a doubt superior to all other monetary policies. It cannot be changed for any reason whatsoever: be it war, economic crisis, or worse, to feed the ego of a politician up for re-election.

CHAPTER 3.
CUTTING OUT THE MIDDLEMAN

Not only does Bitcoin remove the risks of "programmed" inflation, but it also offers an alternative to the banking system as a whole by providing users a solution to the double-spending problem *without needing to resort to a third party*. It's a system of digital cash that allows peer-to-peer cash transactions in cyberspace. This system operates securely without needing the participants to know or trust each other. Bitcoin transactions are fast and final, the digital equivalent of handing over a dollar bill to someone, except remotely, through a digital channel. If I give you a dollar bill (in the real world), you don't need to know who I am in order to receive it. You simply need to ensure that the dollar isn't counterfeit. This is what a cash transaction is all about. When two people use cash to settle a transaction, they don't need to know each other, much less trust each other. An individual shows up with the goods, the other brings cash, the exchange takes place and the transaction is complete. However, if the exchange is done through a digital service like PayPal or a bank, things get more complicated. You can forget about the anonymous part of the transaction, as it requires at least an exchange of email addresses.

THIRD PARTIES AND DOUBLE-SPENDING

Until now, when a transaction was digital, we didn't have much choice other than to rely on third parties or intermediaries. These intermediaries "supervise" the transaction, ensuring that the payment sum is available in your account and that when it is withdrawn, it lands in the beneficiary's account. It also ensures that this sum cannot be "duplicated," meaning that you can't reuse a sum beyond the amount that you actually own. The truth is, when you send $20 to a friend, no dollar bills are physically moved from your account. The transfer is written on a ledger, which then displays the remaining funds in your account. This then brings us to one of the functions of financial intermediaries, which is to prevent a dollar from being used more than once for a given transaction. If an amount leaves bank A and lands on bank B's ledger, bank A ensures that this amount will not be able to be used for another transaction towards bank C. We have no other choice than to trust the banking institution's ledger each time we make a transaction using something other than cash. *Banks and other financial intermediaries are ledgers*; it is a centralized system that you cannot bypass when you make a (digital) fiat transaction.

This intermediary role was indispensable, simply because it was impossible to control the issuance of digital money. Being infinitely duplicatable is part and parcel of digital objects. If you don't believe me, talk to the music industry! When you email a file to a colleague, this creates at least 2 copies of the existing file: one on your computer and the other in the recipient's inbox. Not to mention the copy that exists on your email provider's server, as well as those in the provider's backups, the backups of your computer, the backups of the recipient, and all the other people who were CC'ed in your email. What's more, the recipient can then send as many copies as he wants by emailing his own colleagues! Once a digital object is released into the wild, *it is impossible to limit the proliferation of copies*. Bitcoin offers a solution to this problem, and by solving it, eliminates the need for financial intermediaries.

Bitcoin allows individuals to make peer-to-peer transactions, regardless of distance, all the while guaranteeing the validity of the transactions, without the risks inherent in duplicating and double-spending the digital money. In this way, Bitcoin allows us to hold and exchange value digitally without the use of a third party. This is a technological revolution in and of itself.

THE GENESIS BLOCK'S SECRET MESSAGE

In Bitcoin's genesis block,[16] written in the raw data of the very first block that was mined on the blockchain, we find the following message:

---

16 The genesis block is the first block that was mined on Bitcoin's blockchain.

CUTTING OUT THE MIDDLEMAN

"The Times 03/Jan/2009 Chancellor on the brink of second bailout for banks."

This references a January 3, 2009 headline from the London daily national newspaper, *The Times,* reporting on the bailout of the banks by governments and central banks following the financial crisis of 2008. This comment, forever engraved on the genesis block, casts no doubt on Satoshi's motivations. It's a powerful reminder of the somber consequences of the current lax monetary policies.[17]

---

17 At the end of the book, you will find an interview with Francis Pouliot, who opened my eyes to the fact that this inscription had another use. Indeed, Francis points out that it also serves as a kind of time stamp, proving that the original block was not mined before that date.

CHAPTER 4.
THE TRANSACTIONS AT THE HEART OF BITCOIN

"It is a global distributed database, with additions to the database by consent of the majority, based on a set of rules [...]."

–SATOSHI NAKAMOTO

We now know that Bitcoin allows us to exchange value, digitally, without needing to go through intermediaries. Bitcoin is a large public ledger of digital transactions, and any user can keep a record of all the transactions that ever took place on this ledger.

This chapter is dedicated to studying the mechanisms behind this system. Given their complexity, certain concepts may appear inaccessible at first glance. That is why we'll simplify the aspects of Bitcoin's mechanisms as much as we can without losing accuracy. As a side note, we recommend reading *Inventing Bitcoin* by Yan Pritzker if the contents of this chapter are of particular interest to you.

In the previous chapter, we pinpointed two complications of digital money: the risk of duplication and the risk of double-spending. But how do we prevent these problems *without* going through an intermediary? The first step would be to decentralize the transaction ledger so that it isn't held by a single institution, but by peers on a network instead. Take the example of Philippe and Alice: if Philippe sends $10 to Alice, he informs everyone on the network that he intends to send the money to Alice; everyone must then write the transaction down on their own ledger, the result being a kind of decentralized ledger. The ledger no longer belongs to a single entity: it belongs to the entire network of participants.

This system can work as long as all participants stay trustworthy and keep their records up to date. But what if Alice wants to pay for her morning coffee and croissants with the $10 received from Philippe? Unfortunately, her neighborhood café is not on the network. She could include it, but how does she ensure that they'll respect the rules just like everybody else and refrain from writing all sorts of fraudulent transactions on the ledger?

This is a big problem in computer science: how to ensure that all participants in a network are reliable and honest.

One solution would be to select a trustworthy person—say, Sophie—who will maintain the main ledger and inform all participants of all the transactions so that they can then write them down on their own copies of the ledger. This solution might work for a while. However, if Sophie wants to go on vacation without appointing a replacement, the entire parallel banking system will collapse.

LET'S MAKE A LOTTERY

We could also randomly choose a person who will be in charge of writing the transactions down on the ledger, and then inform the others so that they too can update their own ledgers. This new monetary system would be open to everyone. For it to work, everyone would need to be able to participate. Thus, if Alice wanted to purchase some butter using the $10 that Philippe sent her, then we would need every small business in the neighborhood to be a part of this parallel "banking system"—not just the café. Yet how can everyone participate in the system without anyone being in control? How do we make sure that no one takes advantage of it?

To this point, in his book *Inventing Bitcoin*,[18] Yan Pritzker proposes a

---

18 Yan Pritzker, *Inventing Bitcoin*, 2019.

lottery concept where, in the absence of a central authority, the system needs the following characteristics in order to function properly:

- Each participant needs to be able to create their own lottery ticket.

- It needs to be expensive to participate in the lottery.

- It needs to be very easy for all participants to be able to verify the winning number simply by looking at the ticket.

PROOF-OF-WORK

This new lottery system brings us to the first key concept in Bitcoin: *Proof-of-Work* (PoW). Because anybody can participate in the lottery and create their own lottery tickets, generating the winning number needs to be expensive. Otherwise, anyone could simply generate all the possible numbers and always end up with the winning ticket.

Hence Proof-of-Work, which allows anyone to find the winning number at the cost of considerable energy consumption, as his computers will incur energy costs with the processing power needed to generate billions of numbers before landing on the winning number. Once this winning number is found, the winner earns the right to inscribe onto the ledger the new transactions that others have communicated to him. As a reward, they also obtain freshly-minted bitcoins. We call this process *Bitcoin mining*, which is how new bitcoins are issued.

Bitcoin Node   Neighboring Nodes   Bitcoin Network

A Bitcoin node connected to peers, forming a network.

© Dicoland

But who decides which number is the winner? Long story short, there isn't a single winning number. Instead, there is a ceiling, called the target number, which all participants can calculate independently. When you generate a number that is below this ceiling, you get the privilege to write transactions down on the ledger (in a new block) and get freshly minted bitcoins to compensate for your energy expenditure. The computers connected to the Bitcoin network, called "nodes," calculate the new target number independently, every two weeks; this number depends on the Bitcoin network's hash rate, which is the amount of power deployed by the entire network. Given that all nodes follow the same rules, the result is thus the same for all nodes. We'll come back to this point later, but first, we need to understand some other key Bitcoin concepts: the network, nodes, wallets, keys, addresses, the blockchain, etc.

NETWORK = DECENTRALIZATION

As mentioned earlier, Bitcoin is a network, which is *one* of the reasons why the value of Bitcoin keeps growing. As the network grows, the usefulness and value of the network itself also increase. The more participants exchange bitcoins, the more users accept bitcoins for goods and services, and the greater the network's value. As decreed by Metcalfe's Law, the usefulness of a network is proportional to the square of the number of its users (we'll deal with this subject in more depth in the next chapter).

Bitcoin is a peer-to-peer network, meaning simply that the participants communicate with each other directly, without going through a centralized server. This is essential, as decentralization is at the heart of Bitcoin, the goal being to prevent intermediaries from controlling the whole process.

Computers participating in the Bitcoin network are called *nodes*. A Bitcoin node is simply a computer that executes Bitcoin's open-source software. Every transaction done on the network is repeated on every node, and these nodes are connected to each other. Once the transactions are committed to a block, they stay there for eternity. Anyone can run a node. Thus, nodes as a whole play a fundamental role in decentralizing the network, but no single node is indispensable to keep the network running.

The network keeps track of all submitted transactions by committing them to a *block*. Each block is linked to the existing ones, forming a *blockchain*. In other words, the blockchain is simply a big database that contains all the transactions that ever took place on the network, going all the way back to its creation. As each node keeps its own copy of the blockchain, they are able to enter and leave the network without affecting it. So, to recap:

1. The Bitcoin network is made up of thousands of nodes.

2. Each transaction is repeated to all the nodes. Nodes keep transactions in memory until they are written down on a block, which will then be added to the blockchain.

3. Nodes compete[19] with each other, each looking for the next winning combination (i.e. resolving the PoW problem) to create new blocks and new bitcoins.

4. Once the winning combination is found, the node commits the transactions on a block.

5. Blocks are added and linked together to form the blockchain.

In other words, the Bitcoin network is made up of thousands of interconnected nodes (or miners) that are all on the lookout for the next transactions to be announced on the network. However, you don't need to run a node to use the Bitcoin network, although many hardcore bitcoiners will insist that it is the safest way to participate. In reality, this is rarely the starting point for bitcoiners. Have no fear though; we will see how to run your own node later on.

---

19 We use the term "node" here for simplicity's sake. In order to find the winning combination, users compete through the process of mining, so we should really be talking about "miners." Miners use specialized equipment to find the winning combination.

CHAPTER 5.
THE MECHANISMS AND VALUE OF BITCOIN

"[...] As a thought experiment, imagine there was a base metal as scarce as gold [...] (that) can be transported over a communications channel(.) If it somehow acquired any value at all for whatever reason, then anyone wanting to transfer wealth over a long distance could buy some, transmit it, and have the recipient sell it"

—Satoshi Nakamoto

How can something that no one can see or touch hold value? I often answer this question with the following: "We value trust and yet we can neither see nor touch it." You could call this a rhetorical statement, yet hidden beneath it lies the only reason why fiat money has any value: trust.

This is the paradox behind modern money's value. On the one hand, we have Bitcoin, a virtual form of money that is intangible, but that is truly scarce and limited. On the other, we have fiat money that we can all hold in our hands and whose value is based solely on trust. We have to trust that central banks act in a responsible manner when it comes to their monetary policies, lest the money printing get out of control.

In this chapter, we'll see some factors and mechanisms that give Bitcoin its value.

BITCOIN HAS NO INTRINSIC VALUE

Satoshi Nakamoto posted the following on the bitcointalk.org forum on August 27, 2010:

> *"But if there were nothing in the world with intrinsic value that could be used as money, only scarce but no intrinsic value, I think people would still take up something."*

Bitcoin has no intrinsic value, and that's completely fine. Some will say that the network is what underpins Bitcoin's value; others will tell you that all the energy consumed by miners holds some form of intrinsic value.

But the network doesn't give intrinsic value to Bitcoin. It allows it to assume one of the roles of money, which is to be a medium of exchange. Competition pushing miners to consume energy is essentially Bitcoin's security model. What secures the network and its transactions is the astronomical quantity of energy and equipment required to attack it, not to mention the prohibitive costs. Meanwhile, node operators enforce the very strict emission schedule of newly minted bitcoins. That way, the number of bitcoins in circulation is strictly limited, giving it one of the fundamental characteristics of good money—scarcity. So there we have it: one of the roles, and one fundamental characteristic of good money, transpiring directly from the unique attributes of the Bitcoin network. In Chapter 1, we covered the characteristics of good money, and if you recall, "intrinsic value" was not one of them. Bitcoin has no intrinsic value, and that's a good thing!

In the next pages, we'll touch back on the factors that potentially contribute to Bitcoin's value.

We know that Bitcoin was invented by an individual or group of people under the alias Satoshi Nakamoto. Their anonymity is very important for keeping Bitcoin decentralized, as there can be no CEO, individuals, or organizations that "manage" it. Bitcoin strives and evolves thanks to its contributors and users. This gives the network astonishing resilience in the face of seizures and censorship. No government can pass a law to keep the CEO of Bitcoin accountable. No one can blackmail him to bring about reforms in the network or make it favor one group or another. All because there is no central organization that manages Bitcoin. Bitcoin has no CEO.

What does exist on the network is a few groups with competing interests. For instance, increasing the block size would be very convenient for miners. They could process more transactions, which would haul in much more in transaction fees when they find a new block. However, node operators would find the weight of the blockchain increasing at a higher rate, forcing them to invest considerable sums in bandwidth and equipment to maintain the nodes. Neither has any control over Bitcoin. Developers are free to change any line in the source code, yet nothing forces the miners or node operators to accept the proposed changes. If, for example, miners wanted to unilaterally increase the block size, the node operators refusing the change could very well reject the blocks from those miners. Neither one of these three groups controls Bitcoin. But then, what could motivate them to participate on the network? Developers no doubt participate out of passion, and also to ensure that the bitcoins they hold keep appreciating. Some are also paid by firms that work within the Bitcoin ecosystem. As for the miners, they are motivated by the rewards in mining new coins and processing transactions. Finally, what every node operators wants is the ability to validate transactions themselves, but more importantly, to ensure that the consensus rules are enforced, as their bitcoins would not be as valuable if this were not the case.

AN INFLEXIBLE SUPPLY

Bitcoin's price volatility is spectacular. It isn't rare to see it move 30% in a single day, more than enough to discourage many investors. One of the reasons it fluctuates so much is the Bitcoin market's relatively small size. Bitcoin's total market cap reached the 1 trillion USD mark at the beginning of 2021, before plummeting to as low as a third of this value during the bear market of 2022. A market of that size can still be affected by certain big players known as whales,[20] who are potentially able to move the price on their own. The more the market grows, the harder it becomes for whales to influence the price.

However, the main cause of such fluctuations lies in the fact that the issuance of new bitcoins is completely inflexible. In any other market, the production of a commodity increases when prices go up, and decreases when they go down. These production adjustments go a long way in keep-

---

20 The term "whale" is used to refer to investors who own many bitcoins, and who can therefore potentially influence the market through their actions.

ing prices relatively stable. Just look at crude oil: as soon as OPEC member states decide not to adjust production according to global demand, the impact on prices is immediate. With Bitcoin, we can't adjust production rates, so when demand goes down, prices go down, not production. It's the same thing when demand goes up; since production can't be adjusted to deliver more bitcoins, prices go up. It's that simple! Given that nobody controls Bitcoin, what gets adjusted isn't the production, but the price (and that's a great thing!).

This phenomenon is well summed up in a post that Satoshi published in February 2009 on p2pfoundation.ning.com:

> *"In this sense, it's more typical of a precious metal. Instead of the supply changing to keep the value the same, the supply is predetermined and the value changes."*

BITCOIN'S DIFFICULTY ADJUSTMENT

Now, how does Bitcoin respect its coin emission schedule? As we saw in Chapter 4, the emission of new blocks is insured by a sort of lottery, whereby miners compete with one another to mine the next block and produce new bitcoins. Logically speaking, if more miners join the lottery, then the network's processing power increases, which accelerates the discovery of new blocks, not to mention new coins. It is now time to introduce you to another one of Bitcoin's key concepts: the difficulty adjustment.

The difficulty adjustment happens every 2,016th block (approximately every 2 weeks), which increases or decreases the range of winning numbers. With a larger range of winning numbers, it's easier for miners to mine a block. When the range narrows, it becomes more difficult. This difficulty adjustment ensures that blocks are mined every 10 minutes on average. That's how the Bitcoin protocol adjusts itself depending on the number of miners on the network. Hence the genius of Bitcoin: a system that can self-adjust to hashing power fluctuations, producing a fixed number of coins, without needing any central authority to supervise the process. This concept ensures that the flow of new bitcoins always conforms to the protocol's emission schedule.

METCALFE'S LAW

Metcalfe's Law is a concept first formulated by Robert Metcalfe, founder of 3Com, which allows us to measure network effects. One of the most common examples is the telephone network. It goes without saying that a telephone network with 2 participants won't be as useful as one with millions of users. The law stipulates that a network's usefulness is proportional to the square of the number of its users. In other words, the usefulness and value of a network grows exponentially when its user base increases. Therefore, the more the Bitcoin network grows, the more useful and valuable it becomes.

HASH RATE AND BITCOIN'S VALUE

The hash rate represents the total energy expenditure of all the miners participating in the network's lottery, wanting to obtain the privilege of writing the transactions down on the ledger. We could describe this investment as the cost of generating new bitcoins. What is harder to discern is how much this cost impacts Bitcoin's price on the market. We can imagine that during dips in demand, when the price goes down, some miners may find themself in a situation where they have to sell bitcoins at a loss to pay for their expenses. Other miners will choose to simply hold on to their bitcoins and wait for a more profitable price, betting on Bitcoin's future value, whereas others will decide to shut down operations, consequently lowering the global hash rate. A lower hash rate in turn drops the mining difficulty and makes mining more profitable for those who pressed through. Which is all to say that the total estimated hash rate[21] can give us an idea of how much it costs to generate a bitcoin in any given period.

A VIRTUOUS CYCLE

The higher the price of Bitcoin, the more miners will be enticed to join

---

21 There is no way to calculate the actual power of the network. For an estimate of the total hash power in any given period, you simply count the number of blocks found during that period; you then multiply that number by the total number of possible hashes, then divide it by the number of hashes that are considered valid according to the level of difficulty during this period.

the network. This increases the global hash rate, rendering the network even more secure and attracting investors looking for a store of value, ultimately resulting in higher prices. This growth increases the profitability of miners, hence the virtuous cycle. It must be said that as new miners increase the hash rate, the mining difficulty also goes up, which makes mining less profitable. This coming and going of miners combined with mining difficulty adjustment lead to a certain equilibrium.

CORRELATION WITH THE SEARCH VOLUME

According to an article on decrypt.co,[22] there is a correlation between the search volume for "Bitcoin" on Google and its price. We can then infer that an increase in the search volume is a sign that demand for Bitcoin is rising.

ALL-TIME HIGHS AND THE CAPITULATION OF MINERS

According to data collected and presented by Twitter user @100TrillionUSD,[23] after each all-time high (ATH), Bitcoin's price crashes shortly after. It keeps decreasing until a large number of miners finally capitulate and close down operations. After a decrease in difficulty, mining becomes profitable once again for those who continued to mine, and the price can trend upward again.

HALVING EVENTS AND MONETARY POLICY

A key concept to Bitcoin's emission schedule is the "halving event." As we saw earlier, when a miner wins the lottery and adds a block to the blockchain, they are rewarded with new bitcoins. Given that the number of bitcoins that will ever exist is strictly limited, the strategy that was selected to ensure just that is to emit a certain number of coins at a gradually decreasing rate, until issuance finally ceases completely. That's a good way to avoid shock when the limit is reached. Around the year

---

22 https://decrypt.co/9154/bitcoin-prices-are-80-correlated-with-google-searches

23 https://twitter.com/100trillionUSD/status/1164297159807852547

2140, the Bitcoin network will cease to issue new coins, and transaction fees will replace block subsidies entirely, giving miners a sufficient incentive to invest in mining. This transition will occur very gradually, at the slow and steady pace of the halving events. Transaction fees are already a non-negligible source of income for miners, and the percentage represented by fees in the total revenue for miners will continue to grow until fees completely replace block subsidies in the reward for mining new blocks.

When Bitcoin was launched in 2009, miners received 50 BTC[24] per block. In 2012, after the first halving event, they only received 25 BTC. Next, in 2016, it went down to 12.5 BTC, and at the moment of writing in 2022, the block subsidy is at 6.25 BTC per block.

You will often hear people say that Bitcoin's numbers go up invariably after a halving event. While Bitcoin's historical graph tends to validate this statement, nothing guarantees us that this will always be the case.

This mechanism is the cornerstone of Bitcoin's monetary policy: there will never be more than 21 million bitcoins. In the beginning, 50 bitcoins were created every 10 minutes. This amount is halved every 210,000 blocks thereafter (every 4 years). The gradual decrease of the influx of new bitcoins leads to a deflationary effect on prices, as we saw with the stock-to-flow model.

EVENTS THAT PROVOKED BITCOIN DIPS

- In June 2011, after peaking at around 32 USD, the exchange platform MtGox was hacked and millions of bitcoins were stolen. The price crashed shortly after and it took more than 18 months to recover.

- In April 2013, after a new ATH of 230 USD, MtGox became the victim of a Denial-of-Service attack and temporarily halted operations, resulting in a crash in Bitcoin's price.

- In December 2013, Bitcoin surpassed 1,000 USD. The People's

---

24 BTC—sometimes written XBT—is Bitcoin's symbol.

Bank of China announced that they would forbid financial institutions in China from using Bitcoin. Bitcoin's price subsequently plunged.

- After recovering some of the value lost in December, Bitcoin crashed again after MtGox announced that it would shut down its operations in February 2014.

- Bitcoin finally climbed back up to 1,000 USD in early 2017. The price plunged again when the media reported that China was preparing to ban cryptocurrency exchanges.

- One of the most spectacular price crashes was the crash that followed the ATH of December 2017. The price fell quite abruptly only a few days after reaching a new high of almost 20,000 USD.

- The COVID-19 pandemic did not spare Bitcoin in early 2020. Worth 10,000 USD in February, it dropped below 5,000 USD in March.

- Bitcoin surpassed 60,000 USD in April 2021 before dropping to half of this value following Tesla's successive announcements that it was backing down on its plans to sell its cars in Bitcoin; China also banned Bitcoin (again).

- Bitcoin reached a new ATH in November 2021, exceeding 69,000 USD. It then dropped back below 20,000 USD a few months later in the spring of 2022.

BITCOIN PRICE GRAPH

There is no Bitcoin price graph in this book because they get old pretty fast. However, let's take a look at the following graph, which illustrates in a single image the all-time highs, miner capitulations, halving events, as well as the events that caused Bitcoin to crash.

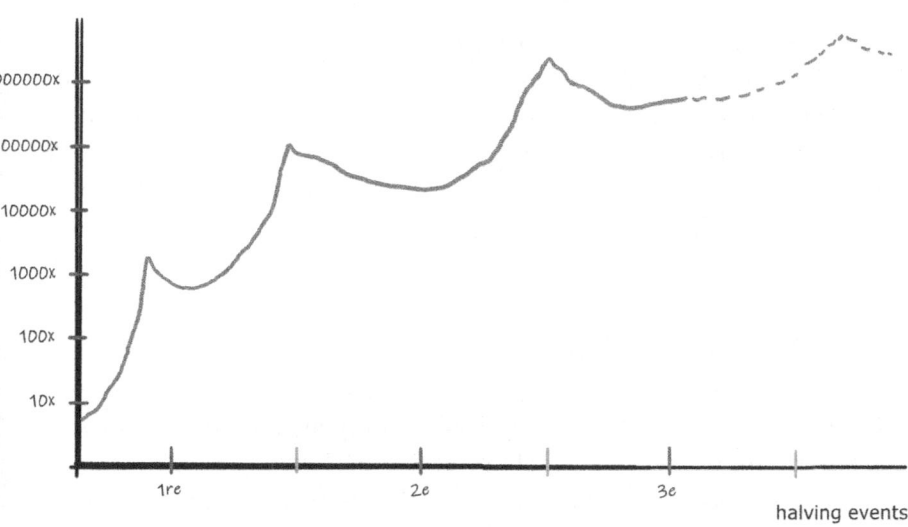

Approximate representation of Bitcoin's price on a logarithmic scale.
The X-axis represents halving events.

I suggest that you read the graph in light of the events described above. Given that we already know halving events happen every 4 years, the first one having occurred in 2012, it shouldn't be too hard to pin the events on the graph.

As you can see, every time Bitcoin reaches a new peak, a dip ensues, followed by another peak. I like to compare this to a canoe with a bow higher than the stern. Every bow represents a new peak, while the center of the boat is the dip that follows. In this graphic, we can clearly distinguish at least two "canoes" between the first and third halving events. The dotted line is what could happen if this trend continues.

A SAFE HAVEN?

A safe haven is an investment characterized by a stable value scarcely affected by market turbulence. Gold is often considered the safe haven of choice, with investors holding on to it in periods of economic instability. Real estate is also considered a safe haven. However, one cannot look over the fact that a safe haven performs better in some situations than in others. The financial crisis of 2008 is a good example. The real estate bubble in the United States clearly contributed to the scale of the crisis. With Bitcoin, this safe haven attribute must still be put to the test. For it to truly be considered a safe haven, Bitcoin's performance has to be uncorrelated to traditional stock markets. Personally, it's the deflationist aspect of Bitcoin's monetary policy that fuels my optimism regarding its value. I think it's safe to say that Bitcoin's monetary policy contrasts with the inflationary aspect of modern monetary policies.

A HEDGE AGAINST INFLATION

On August 11, 2020, the publicly-traded company MicroStrategy (Nasdaq: MSTR) announced the purchase of 21,454 bitcoins for 250 million USD. On this occasion, the company explicitly stated that they considered this "investment" to be a hedge against inflation, especially in the current macroeconomic climate, referencing the sanitary and economic crises of 2020.[25] A few weeks later, in September 2020, MicroStrategy announced that they yet again purchased some more bitcoins, and that they then held 425 million USD worth of BTC. A few days after this announcement, the company's CEO, Michael Saylor, shared his buying strategy on Twitter. So as not to influence the price of Bitcoin too greatly, MicroStrategy made 88,617 transactions over 74 hours, the equivalent of 39,414 USD per minute. Right before 2020 ended, MicroStrategy announced the acquisition of 29,646 more bitcoins, raising the value of their bitcoin holdings in 2020 to over 1 billion USD.[26] And a few weeks later, in February 2021, Tesla Inc. announced the purchase of 1.5 billion USD in bitcoins.[27] It will be very interesting to see in the months and years to come if this trend, started by these companies, will keep on going. As of September 2022, Microstrategy now has almost 130,000 bitcoins, having acquired them at a total price of $3.98 billion.[28]

---

25 https://www.businesswire.com/news/home/20200811005331/en/MicroStrategy-Adopts-Bit-coin-Primary-Treasury-Reserve-Asset

26 https://www.microstrategy.com/en/company/company-videos/microstrategy-announces-over-1b-in-total-bitcoin-purchases-in-2020

27 https://www.bloomberg.com/news/articles/2021-02-08/tesla-bets-1-5-billion-on-bitcoin-in-new-policy-crypto-surges

28 https://www.coindesk.com/business/2022/09/20/microstrategy-now-holds-almost-130k-bitcoin-buys-301-btc/

BITCOIN AS AN INVESTMENT

Although Bitcoin is beyond a shadow of a doubt the best investment of a lifetime for anyone who invested early enough, to me it's more of a savings vehicle. This is mostly just a question of semantics. Nowadays, saving—meaning the act of keeping a part of what we earn in reserve—is a concept that has become less and less popular given the ridiculous interest rates offered by banks, not to mention the effects of inflation. A dollar spent today is worth more than a dollar spent tomorrow. In order to protect their savings for future generations, people have no choice but to turn towards investments, so they can at least beat inflation. Unfortunately, investments come with their fair share of risks.

Currently, Bitcoin could very well be qualified as an investment, given that "investing" in Bitcoin definitely involves risks. Yet my angle on this is more long-term. In my eyes, Bitcoin is the money of the future, at which point people won't be *investing* in Bitcoin but rather *saving* in Bitcoin.

To know more about investing in Bitcoin, I strongly recommend reading *Why Buy Bitcoin* by Andy Edstrom.

Part II
HOW TO USE BITCOIN

CHAPTER 6.
KEYS, WALLETS, AND UTXOS

"[...] a new key pair should be used for each transaction to keep them from being linked to a common owner".

—SATOSHI NAKAMOTO

To use Bitcoin, you don't need to submit your name or post code. What you'll need instead are keys, which serve as identifiers and passwords on the network. It goes without saying that keeping such keys safe is of utmost importance, as they control access to your bitcoins and your transactions history. Simply put, in order to receive bitcoins, you'll need a public key, while a private key will be needed to spend it. Which is why Bitcoin keys come in pairs. Don't let the name fool you, though: you should never share your public key publicly. It needs to be kept secret, as it can be used to retrace every transaction you've ever made. Enter the solution for safeguarding public keys... you simply multiply them.

BITCOIN WALLETS AND ADDRESSES

Generating Bitcoin addresses, which are a sort of disposable public key, is one function of the Bitcoin wallet. A Bitcoin wallet can take the form of a computer program installed on your desktop, an app on your smartphone, a website, or even a piece of paper. The purpose remains the same. Only instead of putting cash into it like a physical wallet, Bitcoin wallets store all the keys needed to query the network about the user's unspent balances, as well as to make Bitcoin transactions, transferring coins from one address to another. The choice of a wallet, not to mention how it is initiated, will be discussed later on.

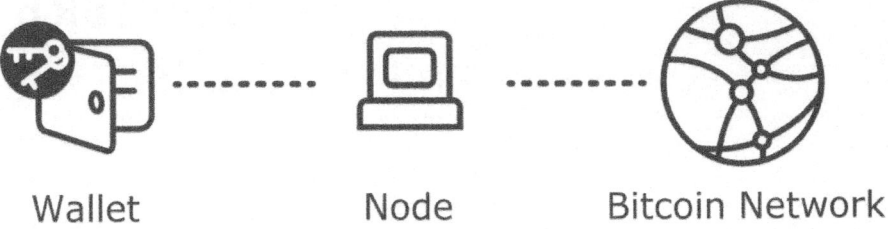

| Wallet | Node | Bitcoin Network |

A wallet containing keys is connected to a node that is itself connected to the Bitcoin network.

Bitcoin addresses look like the following:

myUUXn6LfAm6MN8ae1xkVkthNSjFShQKWd

I strongly recommend using a new address for each new transaction. That way, someone who gains access to a Bitcoin address will only be able to see the single transaction that's linked to the address, rather than the unspent balance of every single transaction that you've ever made, which is something your public key would allow them to do.

| Private Key | Public Key | Bitcoin Addresses |

The wallet contains your private key and uses your public key to generate Bitcoin addresses.

UNSPENT TRANSACTION OUTPUTS: UTXOS

As with most money transfer systems throughout the 20th century, whenever you make a Bitcoin transaction, you communicate information that allows the transfer of bitcoins from one address to another (from the sender to the receiver). In fact, the unspent balance of each transaction sent to addresses generated by your public key is what is used to determine how many bitcoins you have in your wallet. In other words, the "Unspent Transaction Output" (UTXO). For example, let's imagine a fictional wallet that has received three transactions. One of those transactions has already been spent, while the other two still have unspent balances, meaning they are both UTXOs. The following table explains how the unspent balance of our wallet is calculated:

UTXO	Received amount	Spent amount	Balance (UTXO)
Transaction 1	0,003 BTC	-	0,003 BTC
Transaction 2	0,002 BTC	0,002 BTC	
Transaction 3	0,005 BTC	-	0,005 BTC
		Total	0,008 BTC

Now, imagine that a bitcoiner friend gives you a small amount of bitcoin as a gift each year, in the form of paper wallets. He uses the public key of each wallet created on a yearly basis to add a few fractions of a bitcoin to the total amount. In 2020, during Bitcoin's bull run, you start getting interested and meet up with your friend to ask him for help to determine how many bitcoins you own. All he will have to do is hand over the different public addresses of your paper wallets, along with their unspent outputs, like so:

myUUXn6LfAm6MN8ae1xkVkthNSjFShQKWd – 0.01 BTC

mjPrzFr84SRXPTygRGTiWJkQ8SZwNdSd93 – 0.005 BTC

mxgX9zrwQuyQ6Pz6LyBYDwVzxhdcAh6WZB – 0.003 BTC

mtgoRbUoc424NxbLoMamTPYhwS9HBiq5eB – 0.002 BTC

mw9qzMLnGiiuiXZJy3tGYnDbMzqavuWoHs – 0.0075 BTC

mqe6pbyhaYVa1jkKGYBJfG7Hhm9CqMqpHd – 0.0025 BTC

Your friend then suggests that you search for each address[29] on the blockstream.info/testnet[30] website. This will confirm that these addresses have indeed received a total of 6 transactions, for a grand total of 0.03 BTC. After which your friend helps you sweep your paper wallets into another Bitcoin wallet freshly installed on your phone. This involves transferring all the UTXOs from a paper wallet to a mobile wallet, resulting in the balances of the paper wallet's UTXOs being spent to create new UTXOs in your new phone wallet. Here is what such a process looks like:

myUUXn6LfAm6MN8ae1xkVkthNSjFShQKWd – 0.01 BTC

→ **2N5UnUrAdsWX8BfPJrG5J351FDWnhVCdQak** *– 0.01 BTC*

mjPrzFr84SRXPTygRGTiWJkQ8SZwNdSd93 – 0.005 BTC

→ **2MzBCi2Jzf2dxtt6Uprn5jTZNCFu6pQESJ3** *– 0.005 BTC*

mxgX9zrwQuyQ6Pz6LyBYDwVzxhdcAh6WZB – 0.003 BTC

→ **2NBXo4KCkt4c6iG2TKNvv8SPbu1HWqdWkFa** *– 0.003 BTC*

mtgoRbUoc424NxbLoMamTPYhwS9HBiq5eB – 0.002 BTC

→ **2NEmu2MnKA2ct2vwRzqzhTcU9zVsuRsz2dU** *– 0.002 BTC*

mw9qzMLnGiiuiXZJy3tGYnDbMzqavuWoHs – 0.0075 BTC

→ **2MzgHCqTtyPWqHUN8RFx3WRvVJ6eD2DW1LD** *– 0.0075 BTC*

mqe6pbyhaYVa1jkKGYBJfG7Hhm9CqMqpHd – 0.0025 BTC

→ **2MydCQjg7ftPp6rnBdaGaVJ114cfBba8PQL** *– 0.0025 BTC*

Each original address above represents the Bitcoin address of one of 6 paper wallets. Below each address, we see the destination addresses (**in bold**) of the new mobile wallet. These lines sum up the transfer of the funds held in the paper wallets to the new mobile wallet.

---

29 In the Appendix, you will find a QR code for each of these six addresses, allowing you to view them on Blockstream's block explorer.

30 When viewing these transactions on Blockstream's block explorer, you will notice that these addresses contain tBTC instead. These tBTC tokens are test bitcoins traded on the Testnet—Bitcoin's test network. These tokens have no monetary value.

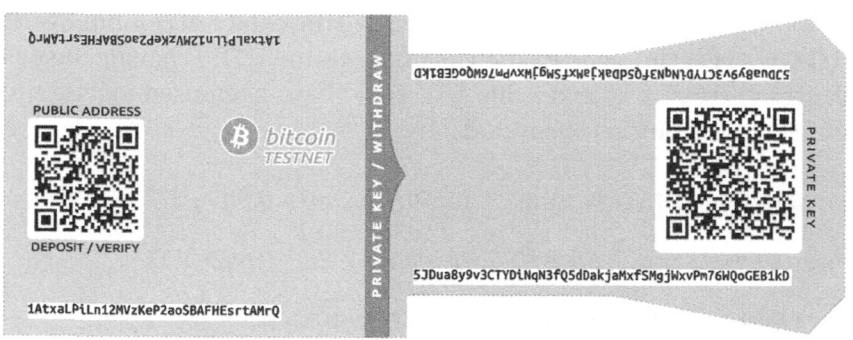

Example of a paper wallet on Bitcoin's Testnet, generated on https://bitcoinpaperwallet.com

As we can see, the paper wallets are simply made up of a public address to which you can send bitcoins and then check the unspent balance, as well as a private key that allows you to sweep the funds onto another, more practical wallet. Paper wallets are not recommended nowadays, as there are methods that are more simple, practical and secure, which will be discussed in the next chapter.

Now, let's say that you decide to test out buying a gift card from your favorite restaurant with 0.005 BTC. Thrilled by the success of your first experiment, you find a service that allows you to pay your bills in bitcoins.[31] After covering the heating bill with 0.01 BTC, your unspent balance now amounts to 0.015 BTC.

For the first transaction, to buy the gift card, your wallet uses the UTXO with an unspent balance of 0.005 BTC:

2MzBCi2Jzf2dxtt6Uprn5jTZNCFu6pQESJ3 – 0.005 BTC

→ **2NA9YcT14V7x7i4UHydH7GgKLU8N9QsXnfw** – *0.005 BTC*

As for the second transaction, for paying the heating bill, your wallet uses the UTXO with an unspent balance of 0.01 BTC:

myUUXn6LfAm6MN8ae1xkVkthNSjFShQKWd – 0.01 BTC

→ **2N5UnUrAdsWX8BfPJrG5J351FDWnhVCdQak** – *0.01 BTC*

---

31 Bylls.com is a service that allows you to pay your bills with your bitcoins.

In both cases, your wallet would have had the choice of combining other UTXOs to get the same result. For instance, the UTXOs having unspent balances of 0.002 BTC and 0.003 BTC could have been used together for the first transaction, as illustrated here:

mtgoRbUoc424NxbLoMamTPYhwS9HBiq5eB – 0.002 BTC

mxgX9zrwQuyQ6Pz6LyBYDwVzxhdcAh6WZB – 0.003 BTC

→ **2NA9YcT14V7x7i4UHydH7GgKLU8N9QsXnfw** *– 0.005 BTC*

But in fact, if you check the transaction details having transferred funds to *2NA9Yct14V7x7i4UHydH7GgKLU8N9QsXnfw,*[32] you'll notice that the wallet decided to combine other transactions instead. This can be explained by the fact that transaction fees need to be taken into account. You'll find the remainder of this example in Appendix 1, where we will introduce transaction fees, dust, and return addresses.

WALLET CHOICE

The Bitcoin wallet is your gateway to the Bitcoin network. This is the software that will allow you to send and receive bitcoins. It will also track all your coins, allowing you to view your Bitcoin balance.

Choosing the "right" Bitcoin wallet is of course crucial for a successful Bitcoin experience. It would be a mistake to underestimate the importance of this step. The one thing that you should definitely not do is search for a wallet in your smartphone's app store and install the first wallet that appears in your search results. New apps related to the Bitcoin ecosystem regularly appear within the various app stores. Separating the wheat from the chaff is not that simple! Generally, when people are introduced to Bitcoin by a friend, they use the same wallet as the one that their friend uses. Another very common pattern is to use the wallets that are embedded within the apps and websites of various Bitcoin exchange platforms. We will see why neither of these solutions is optimal.

When the time comes to choose a Bitcoin wallet, it is preferable to

---

32 In the Appendix, you will find a QR code for this address allowing you to view them on Blockstream's block explorer.

rely on the community of developers and other aficionados, commonly referred to as "peers." In Appendix 2 of this book, you will find more details regarding the importance of verifying the authenticity of the code contained within the files that you download.

For the purposes of this chapter, I chose the Blockstream Green wallet because it contains all the features I wanted to demonstrate. Do not treat this choice as absolute.

QUICK START GUIDE

On your smartphone, open your browser and enter https://blockstream.com/green/ in the URL bar. On this page, you will find a link or a button which will direct you to the Blockstream Green application page in your favorite app store. Once the app is installed on your device, launch it. The following screen should appear:

You can now create your new wallet by pressing the Create New Wallet button.

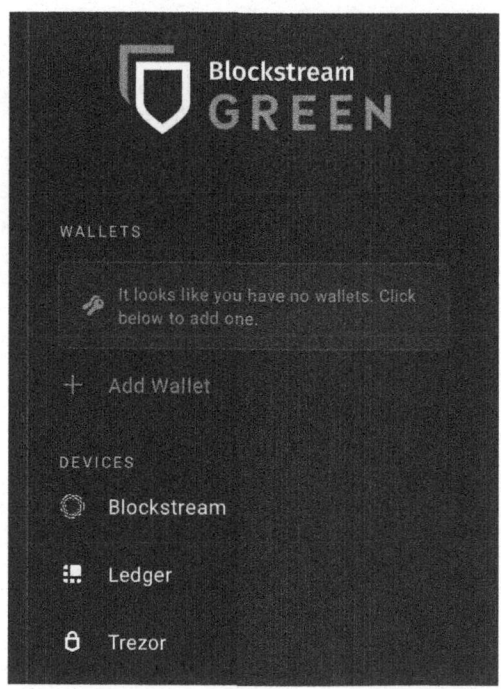

The Blockstream Green wallet's home screen.

New wallet screen.

The next screen should allow you to select the network you want to connect to. For the purposes of this quick start guide, be sure to select "Bitcoin," as this guide is intended to quickly get you some real bitcoins. Later in this chapter, we will connect to another network—the Bitcoin Testnet—and we are going to send some test coins instead of real bitcoins so we won't incur the risk of losing real BTC. **But for now, make sure you choose "Bitcoin."**

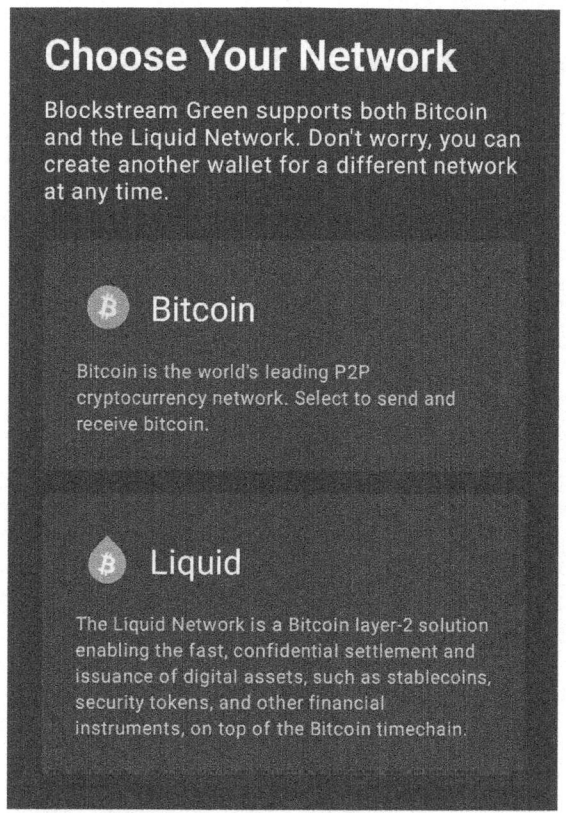

Network configuration screen.

On the next screen, choose "Singlesig." I suggest selecting 24 words for the recovery phrase length.

Choose Security Policy

Once selected, this spending policy cannot be changed. For tips on what type of security is best for you, visit our Help Center.

🔑 Singlesig

Your funds are secured by a single key held on your device. Simpler to set up and operate than multisig. If in doubt, select this option.

🔑 Multisig Shield

Your funds are secured by multiple keys, with one key on your device and another on our servers protected by your 2FA. Select this option for enhanced security.

Recovery phrase length   12 | 24

Security policy screen.

Once you choose "Singlesig," a series of tips and recommendations should appear. It's imperative to follow them or you could lose your bitcoins forever! Mark my words, I'm not saying these things lightly. These recommendations will all be covered in detail below.

In the next step, you will need to write down the 24 words that will make up your mnemonic phrase, or seed phrase. This seed phrase is in fact your private key. It represents the closest thing to "touching" or "seeing" your bitcoins. This series of words allows you to access your bitcoins using any wallet that supports this standard. If, for example, something were to happen to your phone containing your Bitcoin wallet, you would not lose the bitcoins contained in it. Actually, let's take this opportunity to emphasize that your bitcoins are not located in your phone. They are on the blockchain. What your phone contains is the public key that allows you to look at and receive your coins, as well as the private key that allows you to spend them. These 24 words are all you need to "own" your bitcoins.

Here are some recommendations:

1. Clearly and legibly write each word down on a piece of paper.

2. Do not store these words electronically.

3. Do not take any pictures or screenshots of these words.

4. Do not write these words down in a file on your computer. Viruses and spyware specialize in finding these sets of words that give access to bitcoins.

5. Do not store these words on an online service such as Google Drive or Google Doc, or even in a password manager such as 1Password, as someone who would have access to these accounts would also have access to your bitcoins.

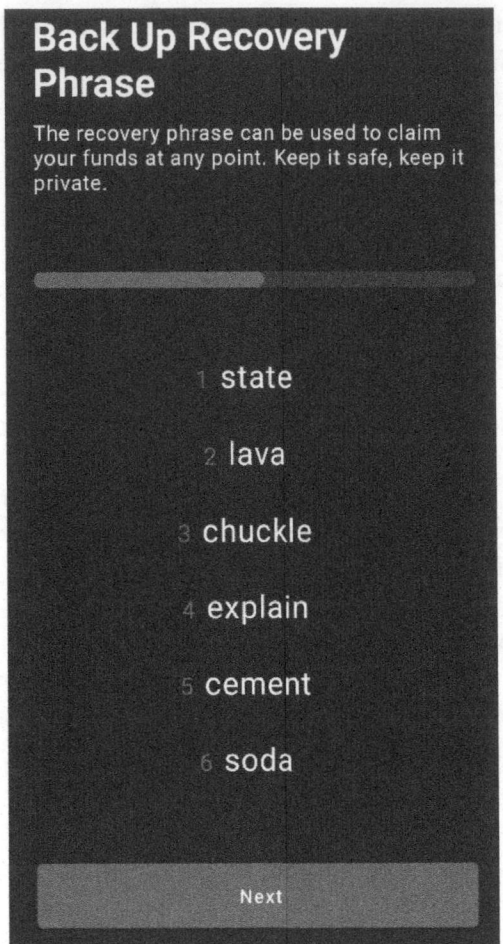

Back Up Recovery Phrase

The recovery phrase can be used to claim your funds at any point. Keep it safe, keep it private.

1 state

2 lava

3 chuckle

4 explain

5 cement

6 soda

Next

One of the screens listing the words of the seed phrase.

I also recommend that you simply write down your 24 words on a piece of paper and keep at least two copies; you could, for instance, keep one in a fireproof safe at home, and the second one in a safe deposit box at the bank. Some experts even advise that you make sure your seed phrase is not visible to your computer's webcam when you write the words down.

The app will ask you to confirm the position of the different words. This step is necessary to ensure that you wrote these words down correctly.

You will then have the opportunity to name your wallet. You will also have the opportunity to set some advanced settings like "connect with Tor." This allows you to hide your IP address. As we saw in Chapter 4, Bitcoin wallets depend on nodes for interacting with the blockchain. By enabling Tor, the node you connect to through your wallet will not know your IP address.

You will then be prompted to create a PIN that will protect your wallet from unauthorized access.

Congratulations! Your wallet is now initialized. You are ready to receive your first bitcoins!

Receiving Bitcoins

By pressing the receive button, you will now enter the screen for setting up a QR code for receiving bitcoins. You can now copy your new Bitcoin address, for example 3PzdxXoERZAJ5tFZPofykbFenoAMLugAUK, by simply tapping it and pasting it into a text message for the person who wants to send you bitcoins. Obviously, **do not send bitcoins to the address written above, as your bitcoins will be lost! Use your own address!**

Main account screen.

If you and the person who wants to send you bitcoins are in the same room or chatting on a video call, you could also use the QR code. Their wallet will be able to use their phone's camera to capture your Bitcoin address by scanning your phone screen. A field for setting the desired amount is also available in the "More Options" menu. This field adds the specified amount at the end of the address, allowing you to simultaneously communicate the address as well as the amount to be sent, as such:

bitcoin:3PzdxXoERZAJ5tFZPofykbFenoAMLugAUK?amount=0.002

Now that you have completed all these steps, you can receive bitcoins in your wallet. You could use an online exchange right now, get your first bitcoins and send them to an address belonging to your brand new Bitcoin wallet. We'll come back to this later in more detail.

Receiving address.

Systematic Use of New Addresses

The importance of using a new address for each Bitcoin transaction cannot be stressed enough. At first glance, a new user might be tempted to use the same address over and over again, much like using an email address. Or he might be tempted to use a few different addresses to segment the sources. For example, one address to receive his pay cheque; one address to receive bitcoins from a friend; one address to receive bitcoins from exchange #1; another one for exchange #2... This could be very convenient to keep track of where all the bitcoins are coming from.

The problem with this method is that since Bitcoin's blockchain is public, a person who knows one address will be able to look up the balance, as well as all the transactions made to and from that address. There are even companies that specialize in collecting this information and selling it to the highest bidder. A better way to identify transactions would be to add a description label to each transaction in the wallet.

Furthermore, if you send $200 in ten transactions to ten different addresses, the balance associated with each of those addresses will be ten times less attractive to a potential thief.

Let's now project ourselves into the not-so-distant future in which you are paid in bitcoins and you have convinced your landlord to accept bitcoins as payment for your rent. You've given the payroll service a Bitcoin address, and every two weeks, your pay cheque is deposited there without hassle.

When your landlord starts to trace the transaction history of all the payments you ever sent him, he will notice that in one of the addresses you use, a recurring amount of a few thousand dollars is deposited every two weeks. That's all it takes for your landlord to guess that this is your salary. A few weeks later, he will notice a substantial increase in this amount. He will deduce that you have probably been promoted. A month later, when you renew your lease, your landlord may be tempted to take advantage of your promotion by inflating your rent.

The transparency of the Bitcoin blockchain is desirable and necessary. Being able to look at every transaction and know their balance allows us to track the full inventory of existing bitcoins at any time. This can be useful when, for example, a non-profit organization wants to organize a donation campaign and wants the total donations to be publicly known. Conversely, an entrepreneur who sells a product over the Internet would be unwise to post a Bitcoin address on her website for the purpose of accepting Bitcoin payments. Anyone could inspect the transactions linked to that address and find out how much that entrepreneur is making.

Thus, in order to prevent transactions from being traced, any individual or business wishing to accept Bitcoin payments can use a platform like BTCPay Server.[33] Instead of simply providing an address to your customer or donor, BTCPay Server presents itself as an interface that will allow the user to pay in bitcoins, generating a new Bitcoin address for each new transaction.

Restoring a Green Wallet

As I mentioned earlier, your Bitcoin wallet allows you to receive and send coins, but it doesn't really contain your bitcoins. Your wallet contains the keys that give you access to your bitcoins, which are actually located on the blockchain. So, fortunately, if you lose your wallet, your bitcoins will not be lost. You can recover your keys using the seed phrase that the wallet generated for you when it was initialized. So if you lose access to your wallet, you can simply take your seed phrase out of hiding and restore your wallet. Here's how: on your new phone, install the Blockstream Green application. When you open the app, you will be presented with a screen that offers you the option of creating or restoring a wallet. After you choose the "Restore" option, make sure you choose the right network. If you want to restore a wallet on the Bitcoin network, select the Bitcoin network. For the Testnet, select the Testnet network.

Now enter the 24 (or 12) words from your seed phrase. You will then be asked to create a PIN to protect access to your wallet. That's it! It's that easy!

---

33 https://btcpayserver.org/

Enter your recovery phrase

1 follow	2 that	3 rabbit
4 into	5 that	6 hole
7 great	8 fortune	9 will
10 come	11 when	12 you
13 hold	14 what	15 you
16 own	17 assume	18 nothing
19 always	20 verify	21 other
22 fork	23 equal	24 garbage

12	24

Seed phrase restoration.

Different Types of Wallets

There are several types of wallets. In this book, we've already mentioned and used paper wallets, as well as the mobile wallet provided by Blockstream. There are also desktop wallets that you can install on your computer, wallets that are integrated directly into exchanges, and hardware wallets. There are also hot and cold wallets. Hot storage refers to wallets whose keys are stored on a device that has access to the Internet, allowing quick access to funds. Cold storage refers to a form of key storage that is not connected to the Internet, such as with the Coldcard[34] hardware wallet. A very important fact to note here is that in order for a private key to be considered as "being kept in cold storage," it must not

---

34 https://coldcardwallet.com

only be kept on a device that is disconnected from the Internet, but it must also have been generated by a device that does not have access to the Internet. An air-gapped device like the Coldcard can do just that. A proper cold storage process is usually reserved for fairly large amounts of bitcoins that you want to hold on to over a long period of time. There are intermediate means that combine good protection and relative ease of use. We'll come back to this briefly in the next section.

Best Practices

To conclude this chapter, we will try to briefly present the best practices regarding the use, protection, and retention of your keys. In particular, we will cover the concepts of hardware wallets, the importance of entropy, transaction anonymization, the use of BTCPay for receiving payments, and finally, we will discuss strategies for securing your keys and the importance of estate planning.

Not Your Keys, Not Your Bitcoin

One of the risks associated with using a wallet is key management. A multitude of problems could occur. If you use an online wallet provided by your exchange platform, you run the risk of seeing the platform cease their operations overnight, cutting off access to your coins. As they say in the industry: "Not your keys, not your bitcoin." Some people still prefer to leave their tokens with a third party—their exchange platform, for instance—precisely so that they don't need to manage their keys. If you do this, you must have blind trust in that third party. Examples abound of exchanges that have stolen or lost their depositors' bitcoins. I personally came close to losing my meager bitcoin holdings when QuadrigaCX fell in 2018. My tokens were in their possession until I got myself a Trezor.[35] The Trezor wallet was the first hardware wallet to hit the market back in 2014. Had I not acquired it in late 2018, I—like many other Canadians— would have lost all my bitcoins.

Hardware Wallets

Hardware wallets are small electronic devices that usually have a

35 https://trezor.io

screen, a USB port, and a few buttons. They plug into your computer or phone through a USB cable or Bluetooth connection. These devices allow you to generate and store your keys directly on the device.

TrezorOne hardware wallet
(source: SatoshiLabs).

When you install a desktop or mobile wallet, when you write down the seed phrase, and when you generate a Bitcoin address to send tokens to, you trust that the developer of that application didn't add any malicious code that would allow them to steal your keys. This is exactly why most Bitcoin wallet software and applications are open-source, so that the code can be audited to make sure it doesn't contain malicious code that could potentially communicate your private keys to a third party. This is precisely the problem that hardware wallets address. They keep your keys safe. They never share your private keys with your mobile or desktop wallet. Most of these devices rely on a desktop software wallet to initialize and perform transactions. This is one of the major flaws of the two most popular hardware wallets. They both depend on a software wallet provided by the manufacturer. This wallet necessarily communicates the wallet's public key to the manufacturer's servers in order to display the balance of your UTXOs. New products now exist that completely bypass this problem. They are however less easy to use than the most popular hardware wallets at the moment. Notwithstanding the problem of sharing your public key, it is still much safer to use a Trezor or a Ledger[36] than to leave your tokens on an exchange platform or on your phone.

THE IMPORTANCE OF ENTROPY

Beyond the hazards of key management, there may also be risks related to the lack of entropy during the generation of your keys. When you generate your Bitcoin keys, it is imperative that a fair amount of randomness enter the recipe behind the creation of your keys. If the device that generates your keys has too little entropy, it could prove fatal to the confidentiality of your private keys. The best example to illustrate this risk occurred in 2013 when a bug was discovered in the Java SecureRandom class.[37] This anomaly in Android's random number generator resulted in the security of keys generated by a portion of the available Bitcoin mobile wallets at the time being compromised. In order to understand this without getting into too many technical details, try to wrap your head around the fact that the total number of Bitcoin keys and addresses that can ever be generated is in the order of magnitude of the total number of atoms in the universe. But that's only if the key generator is given a sufficiently random number. If the provided number is not random enough, it reduces the range of possibilities to a mere fraction of this. Some hackers at the time sensed the potential attack vector on Android Bitcoin wallets, and thus generated and tested the balance of a myriad of Bitcoin private keys. With the scope of possibilities greatly reduced, some private keys were compromised and some wallets were emptied. It is therefore important that the modern Bitcoin wallet, regardless of the platform, provide the entropy necessary for secure key generation. Some people even use good old-fashioned dice rolls to generate enough entropy themselves. After reading this paragraph, you might wonder what would prevent someone from generating all the possible Bitcoin private keys? The answer is actually quite simple... There wouldn't even be enough atoms in the universe to save them all,[38] and that's not to mention the amount of energy it would

36 https://www.ledger.com
37 https://arstechnica.com/information-technology/2013/08/google-confirms-critical-android-crypto-flaw-used-in-5700-bitcoin-heist
38 Assuming 1 bit per atom.

take to generate them, or even the time it would take to do so. Let's just say that all the energy trapped in our sun and the five billion years it has left to shine would not be enough. But for this to be true, the keys must be generated with enough entropy.

ANONYMITY AND BITCOIN

As we have already seen, Bitcoin is by no means a particularly private system. Although you do not have to provide your personal information to use it, its use leaves digital traces that are then recovered by specialized companies that resell or share this information with governments and various other entities.[39] As soon as you deal with an exchange platform to buy or sell your bitcoins, most jurisdictions impose the notions of anti-money laundering compliance and "know your customer" (AML and KYC). This means that their customers must provide certain pieces of personal information to allow exchanges to identify them and monitor suspicious behavior. This is one situation where your real identity could be linked to some of the Bitcoin addresses you use. Once this information is in the hands of these blockchain analysis companies, anyone interested in your Bitcoin holdings could pay these companies and gain access to this information. There are very sophisticated ways to provide a certain level of anonymity to Bitcoin transactions today. The desktop Wasabi Wallet[40] incorporates the CoinJoin feature that, when used, ensures that transactions are mixed with those of dozens of other users to muddy the waters and prevent anyone from tracking your transactions.

After a few iterations through this mixing tool, it will be impossible for even the sharpest detective to trace your footsteps. People often tend to overlook the importance of anonymity, but as we've already seen in the example of the snooping landlord, you don't need to have anything serious to hide for you to want more anonymity. This kind of service will certainly democratize and become easier to use in the near future. In this way, it could be possible for a larger share of Bitcoin's network users to enjoy a higher level of anonymity.

---

39 https://twitter.com/brian_armstrong/status/1282106176000233472?s=20
40 https://wasabiwallet.io/

RECEIVING PAYMENTS VIA BTCPAY

Although configuring and using BTCPay Server is beyond the scope of this book, I wanted to briefly discuss this topic. BTCPay Server offers a solution to the problem of reusing Bitcoin addresses. Someone who wants to sell products over the Internet might find it laborious to manually generate new addresses in their wallet for each transaction. That's what BTCPay Server takes care of. When a customer is ready to send funds, BTCPay Server generates a new address and communicates it to the customer.

BTCPay Server's payment screen
(image from btcpayserver.org).

"PAYMENT CODES" (PAYNYMS)

In the not-so-distant future, we should see the emergence of initiatives like PayNyms that will allow you to generate a unique "payment code" that never changes and that can be shared publicly without revealing the addresses that are linked to transactions sent to that payment code. These new techniques will likely be democratized as wallets become increasingly compatible with them. In my opinion, we will probably not have to deal with Bitcoin addresses anymore, as simpler solutions will soon emerge—hopefully, anyway.

STRATEGIES FOR SECURING PRIVATE KEYS

If there's one topic in Bitcoin that shouldn't be taken lightly, it's securing your seed phrase; but rest assured, it doesn't have to be particularly complicated. The level of effort put into securing your seed phrase will of course depend on the amount of BTC that is at stake. That said, any amount of BTC, no matter how small, deserves at least some protection.

In my opinion, the bare minimum looks like this: you should have two copies of your seed phrase, handwritten on two pieces of paper, and kept in two separate places. These places must obviously be safe and secure, as if someone were to stumble upon your 24 words, they could steal all your bitcoins!

Some wallets offer a solution to limit this risk by adding a 25th word (preferably a phrase) when creating the seed. You will, of course, not keep this 25th word among the others. You can keep it hidden somewhere else. This is a great way to protect your seed phrase from unauthorized access. However, if you forget or lose this 25th word, you will also lose access to your coins. This 25th word can also have another interesting use: you can set up different accounts with different words. That way, if someone were to force your hand in a $5 dollar wrench attack, you could strategically give them your seed phrase with a 25th word that points to an account with a low balance.

Comic strip by xkcd - https://xkcd.com/538/

To protect your sheet of paper containing your seed phrase, you could keep it in a fireproof and waterproof box, or better, use a metal plate that was specifically designed for this purpose, e.g. the SEEDPLATE by Coinkite.[41]

Another way to store and protect access to your bitcoins is to use a multisignature (or multisig) scheme. Some wallets or services allow you to create multiple keys to back your wallet, requiring a certain number of these keys to be provided in order to spend the bitcoins. For example, a 2-of-3 multisig scheme would allow you to spend your bitcoins even if you lost one of the keys, and likewise would not allow a thief to spend your bitcoins if he only discovered one of your keys. This technique also allows Bitcoin to be used in businesses, requiring at least two signatories to confirm a transaction, thus preventing a cheating employee from running off with the funds.

ESTATE PLANNING

This is a topic that can be tricky and uncomfortable for some people, but when you own bitcoins, it's imperative to prepare for the possibility

---

41 https://coinkite.com

of your own demise. There have probably been too many occasions in which bitcoiners have died unexpectedly without being able to pass on their bitcoins to their loved ones.

Unfortunately, I don't have a magic formula here, as each of the solutions that will be mentioned involve risks. The simplest solution would be to inform a trusted family member that you have bitcoins and provide them with detailed instructions on how to recover them. Of course, the risk here is easy to recognize. Sometimes, you find out too late that the people you trusted didn't deserve that level of trust.

A more sophisticated solution might involve a family member in addition to a third party, such as your attorney, as well as a multisig scheme. You would be able to set the system up in such a way that your significant other could retrieve your funds with his or her key in addition to your lawyer's. The problem here, of course, is that this system could allow your spouse and lawyer to potentially plot against you and "disappear" with your coins!

You could also include a document with the information needed to retrieve your tokens as an attachment to your will. For example, this document could reveal how to retrieve your seed phrase hidden inside your home, as well as your 25th word hidden in another location.

Casa offers an inheritance plan that you can find here: https://keys.casa/bitcoin-inheritance-plan.

CHAPTER 7.
OWNING AND SENDING BITCOINS

"It might make sense just to get some in case it catches on. If enough people think the same way, that becomes a self fulfilling prophecy."

—SATOSHI NAKAMOTO

Now that we've covered the basics of choosing a good Bitcoin wallet and emphasized the importance of properly storing and securing your seed phrase, we're ready to start making Bitcoin transactions, for both buying and selling purposes. When we say "bitcoins" we are simply talking about Bitcoin tokens, which are the UTXOs[42] we discussed previously. So when someone says "my bitcoins," they're referring to the transactions, on the blockchain, containing balances that have not yet been used, and that they have control of through the keys held in their wallet. You should also be aware that you can obtain a mere fraction of a bitcoin.

In this chapter, we will explore the different ways to send and receive bitcoins. It's important to mention that this book, and especially this chapter, are not an inducement to buy bitcoins, and my words should not be construed as financial advice. Will Bitcoin continue to grow, or will its price collapse? No one knows. In my personal opinion, in light of Bitcoin's characteristics and human beings' historical tendency to always choose

---

42 "Unspent Transaction Output".

the hardest currency available to them, I would bet on the former rather than the latter.

The goal is to help you understand how and why Bitcoin is a space for freedom. The idea here is not to buy bitcoins at $10,000 and resell them when the price doubles, triples, or even quintuples,[43] but to allow people to freely choose their currency. It's about having a currency that does not systematically lose 2% of its value every year.[44] It's about having a currency that no government can arbitrarily decide to inflate while making the savers foot the bill;[45] a currency on which no withdrawal limit can be imposed, nor savers' bank accounts raided to fund government debt.[46]

Everyone benefits from using Bitcoin; this is true no matter when you discover it and no matter what its price. It's never "too late" to discover Bitcoin. That's a slogan that charlatans use to sell you their junk cryptocurrencies. If it is indeed too late for Bitcoin, then ask yourself why they are so keen to exchange their worthless tokens for your bitcoins? It's worth asking the question, don't you think? I'll come back to the topic of other cryptocurrencies in Chapter 8.

MINING

To get bitcoins in a relatively easy way, my first recommendation would be to mine them. Although Bitcoin mining has long since stopped being a profitable operation for individuals—as it requires large investments—some services allow you to rent the power of your computer to third parties who will then use it to mine all kinds of cryptocurrencies (altcoins). The beauty of this concept is that *you* get paid in bitcoins. I personally use NiceHash[47] to make my computing power, supported by a very powerful graphics card, available to a buyer's market. The NiceHash application automatically chooses the best offer on the market as well as the best mining algorithm for your particular situation, and provides the

---

43 I find it very interesting that between the time when I was writing this chapter for the first (French) edition of this book, and the date of its publication in 2021, this actually happened.

44 https://www.bankofcanada.ca/core-functions/monetary-policy

45 See the section on Zimbabwe in Chapter 2.

46 https://www.cnn.com/2013/03/19/business/cyprus-deposit-tax-robbery

47 https://www.nicehash.com

buyer with your computer's power in exchange for BTC. This system allows me to heat my basement in winter while receiving BTC in exchange... because one should not underestimate the amount of heat released by a mining computer. My computer easily uses 400 watts of power when it's mining. This is a fact that you should definitely consider before piling up three or four powerful computers in a corner of your house to start mining. You will be surprised at how hot it will get in the room after only a few hours. Furthermore, if you mine in the summer and this heat input requires more air conditioning for your house, your electricity bill will end up being huge!

In my experience, one or two powerful machines in the basement during the winter is the most you can expect without a sophisticated heat removal system. And don't expect to get tons of BTC; the returns will be quite modest. It varies a lot depending on the market, the number of machines you use, and the power of your graphics cards. To give you an idea, mining at my home with two computers this winter (2019–2020), I was probably only making the equivalent of a few dollars a day.[48] And it isn't pure profit either, since it mostly covers the electricity cost. So where's the reward, I hear you ask? The reward lies in the fact that I have to spend that energy to heat my basement anyway. By passing the electrons through a microchip instead of a radiator element, I receive the value of that transferred energy in the form of BTC while heating up my home.

We can nonetheless question the ethical aspect of this process. We must understand that we are taking advantage of the hopes that some people place on a cryptocurrency other than Bitcoin, thinking it will increase in value sufficiently to compensate for their purchases of hash power. I'll let you judge the ethics of this approach. Take note that according to the Canada Revenue Agency, you may be taxed on your mining income depending on whether this activity is personal (a hobby) or commercial. This is decided on a case-by-case basis.[49] Please refer to your country's tax laws for more information.

---

48 To illustrate the wide variability in this market, for the winter of 2020-2021, it was more like ten dollars for the same configuration.

49 https://www.canada.ca/en/revenue-agency/programs/about-canada-revenue-agency-cra/compliance/digital-currency/cryptocurrency-guide.html

REWARD PROGRAMS

An easy and free way to get BTC is to sign up for reward programs that offer bitcoins instead of loyalty points or cash back on purchases. This is a booming industry and many companies are jumping on the bandwagon right now. For example, the Coinmiles application,[50] available in Canada and France, offers the option to receive BTC rewards whenever you make online and in-store purchases. To take advantage of these rewards, simply download the app on your phone, tap on a participating retailer's offer and complete a purchase on their website, or in person at their store. It's a low-cost, no-risk way to get started with bitcoin ownership. In the US, Lolli lets you earn rewards at over 10,000 different stores.

BUYING BITCOINS

There are several ways to purchase bitcoins. Whether it's through a Bitcoin ATM, an app, an exchange platform or an in-person transaction, each of these methods has certain pros and cons.

Bitcoin ATMs

You can find Bitcoin ATMs in most major cities. An interesting advantage of buying BTC at a Bitcoin ATM is that you don't need to identify yourself (for now). Some ATMs will offer the option of generating a paper wallet as a delivery method. If you choose this option, be sure to sweep the funds from the paper wallet into your own wallet as soon as possible. There is no guarantee that it is not compromised in some way. Buying bitcoins through a Bitcoin ATM is generally more expensive than on an exchange platform though. This difference is likely due to the extra transportation and management costs that are required to offer this service.

LocalBitcoins.com

LocalBitcoins allows you to buy and sell bitcoins directly from other users of the service. Users can post their offers to buy or sell directly on the website. LocalBitcoins uses a trusted third-party system to ensure that

---

50 https://coinmiles.io

the BTC fund is only released if the money has been properly received. If you ever sell bitcoins on this site, always keep in mind that a buyer can report the transaction to his bank as fraudulent and the transfer could be reversed.[51]

Other P2P methods for advanced users who wish to purchase non-KYC bitcoins include, but are not limited to: Bisq, Hodl Hodl, Peach, and Robo-Sats. Do your own research before using such services, and understand the risks involved.

Exchange Platforms

Exchanges are probably the best way to get bitcoins for beginners. An exchange platform is a service that allows users to buy or sell bitcoins. Some exchanges allow you to place bids to buy or sell bitcoins. All this activity sets a market price which some buyers then use to make their purchases.

Depending on the jurisdiction in which you are located, the exchange may or may not ask you to provide information regarding your identity, sometimes including an official document, e.g. a driver's license. Exchanges are required to collect such information to comply with anti-money laundering laws and "know your customer" (AML & KYC) guidelines. In France, Coinhouse[52] will ask you for an ID, a passport from the SEPA zone, or a European residence permit. In Quebec, some exchanges can also validate your identity through credit bureaus.

Most exchanges offer to keep your bitcoins in their wallet. Thus, they are custodial platforms. This is of course quite convenient since you don't have to set up another wallet. The problem is that you don't truly own these coins since you don't own the private keys. If something were to happen to the exchange, you could very well lose your coins. Exchanges have lost their users' coins many times in the past, for all sorts of reasons. And believe me, it will happen again. Other exchanges do not keep your bitcoins; these are non-custodial exchange platforms. When you make a purchase, these exchanges send your new coins directly into your own wallet, the one to which only you have the keys. Examples of this would be

---

51 https://medium.com/@Fiach_dubh/psa-canadian-localbitcoins-com-users-e-transfer-scam-warning-f95eef46d3d3

52 https://www.coinhouse.com/

© Dicoland

Bull Bitcoin in Canada or StackinSat in France. In the US, Swan Bitcoin lets you auto-withdraw your funds to your own wallet when your holdings on their platform reach a certain threshold which you can configure yourself.

The concepts that will be covered in the next section typically apply to all exchanges. You will be able to replicate this process on other exchanges operating in your country. I chose to demonstrate the act of purchasing BTC on Bull Bitcoin since I find their process to be relatively simple, and it is a non-custodial exchange.

Go to https://bullbitcoin.com and choose the option to buy bitcoins. When you create an account, you will be asked to verify your identity. The verification process may take some time. You can then press the "Fund Your Account" button to make an Interac transfer and send funds to the exchange. Enter the desired amount for the deposit and then follow the instructions to complete the Interac transfer. Please allow a few hours for the deposit to be processed.

INTERAC E-TRANSFER

Amount you spend	500.00	🇨🇦 CAD
Payment processor fee	- $0.00 CAD	
Flat fee	- $0.00 CAD	
Amount you receive	500.00	🇨🇦 CAD

At current bitcoin rate of $27,624.31 CAD, this would get you

₿0.01812500 BTC.

$ Create funding order

Bull Bitcoin's deposit screen.

Once the deposit is made, you can tap the "Buy Bitcoin" button. You will then need to enter an amount and specify a Bitcoin address that you will have generated beforehand (see Chapter 6). Once you submit the order, the BTC will be transferred to your address.

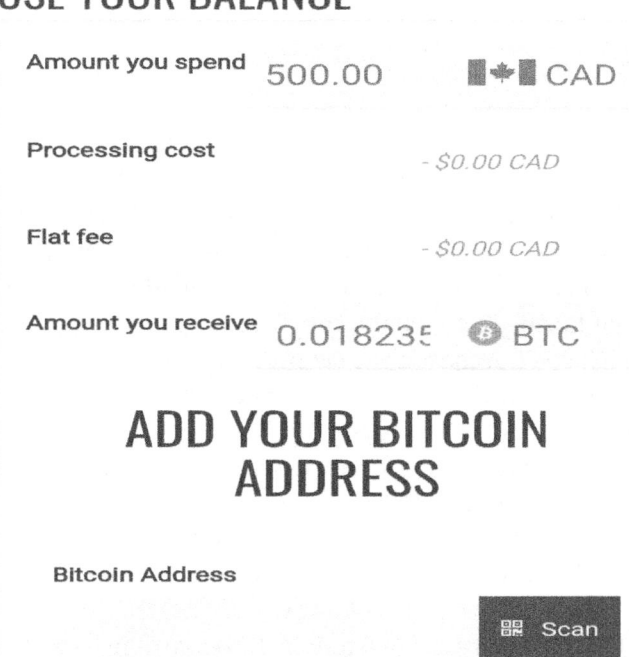

USE YOUR BALANCE

Amount you spend	500.00	CAD
Processing cost		- $0.00 CAD
Flat fee		- $0.00 CAD
Amount you receive	0.018235	BTC

ADD YOUR BITCOIN ADDRESS

Bitcoin Address

Scan

Bull Bitcoin's BTC purchase screen.

Applications

Some exchanges offer their services through an app on your phone. In Canada, Shakepay is a great example. It is indeed one of the easiest and fastest ways to get bitcoins. You can download the application at https://shakepay.com. Cash App is another mobile payment service available in the US and the UK that allows users to purchase bitcoins. You can download the application at https://cash.app/.

Dollar-Cost Averaging

Dollar-Cost Averaging (DCA) is, in my opinion, the best answer to the neverending question: "Is this the right time to buy bitcoins?" By buying bitcoins regularly, and spreading your purchases over a longer period, you minimize the risk of buying at the wrong time. Bull Bitcoin offers this service in Canada: https://bullbitcoin.com/recurring-buys. In France, you can use StackinSat: https://stackinsat.com. Swan Bitcoin offers recurring buys in the US: https://www.swanbitcoin.com/.

TAXES

In Canada, you cannot be taxed for owning cryptocurrencies. In other words, acquiring bitcoins and simply holding onto them is not a taxable event. On the other hand, if you were to sell them, donate them, exchange them for other cryptocurrencies, or use them to purchase property, these actions are considered to be taxable.[53] For individuals, half of the capital gains will be taxed. To calculate your capital gains, simply subtract the price at which you purchased the cryptocurrency from the price at which you sold it. If you paid $150 for your coins when you initially bought them, and they are worth $200 when you sell them, then the capital gain is $50. In France, capital gains are referred to as "*plus-values*." And it seems that exchanging "crypto-assets" between one another is not taxable.[54] Another interesting fact is that in France, you must declare your digital asset accounts held within companies located outside of France.[55]

For the US, here is an excerpt from the IRS regarding virtual currencies:[56]

> *"The sale or other exchange of virtual currencies, or the use of virtual currencies to pay for goods or services, or holding virtual currencies as an investment, generally has tax consequences that could result in tax liability."*

Keep in mind however that all this information will probably age very poorly. It's important to keep up to date with the tax news in your country and to seek professional advice. Please also note that the information provided in this section should not be construed as professional advice.

---

53 https://www.canada.ca/en/revenue-agency/programs/about-canada-revenue-agency-cra/compliance/digital-currency/cryptocurrency-guide.html

54 https://www.legifrance.gouv.fr/affichCodeArticle.do?idArticle=LEGIARTI000038612228&-cidTexte=LEGITEXT000006069577&dateTexte=2019052

55 https://www.legifrance.gouv.fr/affichCodeArticle.do?cidTexte=LEGITEXT000006069577&idAr- ticle=LEGIARTI000006306944

56 https://www.irs.gov/businesses/small-businesses-self-employed/virtual-currencies

SENDING BITCOINS

To get started with sending bitcoins, I suggest you first experiment on the Testnet. The first step in attempting to send tBTC[57] is to follow the instructions outlined in the quick start guide in Chapter 6, but on the Testnet instead. On Blockstream Green's home screen, you can select "App Settings" in the bottom right corner. On the App Settings screen, you will now enable the Testnet. Then, exactly as described in the aforementioned quick start guide, from the home screen, you will tap the "Create a new wallet" button, but this time, you will choose the Testnet network. The rest is exactly as described in the quick start guide. You write the 24 words down, answer the questions, and choose a PIN. *Be sure to keep in mind that these 24 words are for the Testnet; do not confuse them with your Mainnet seed phrase which gives access to your real bitcoins.*

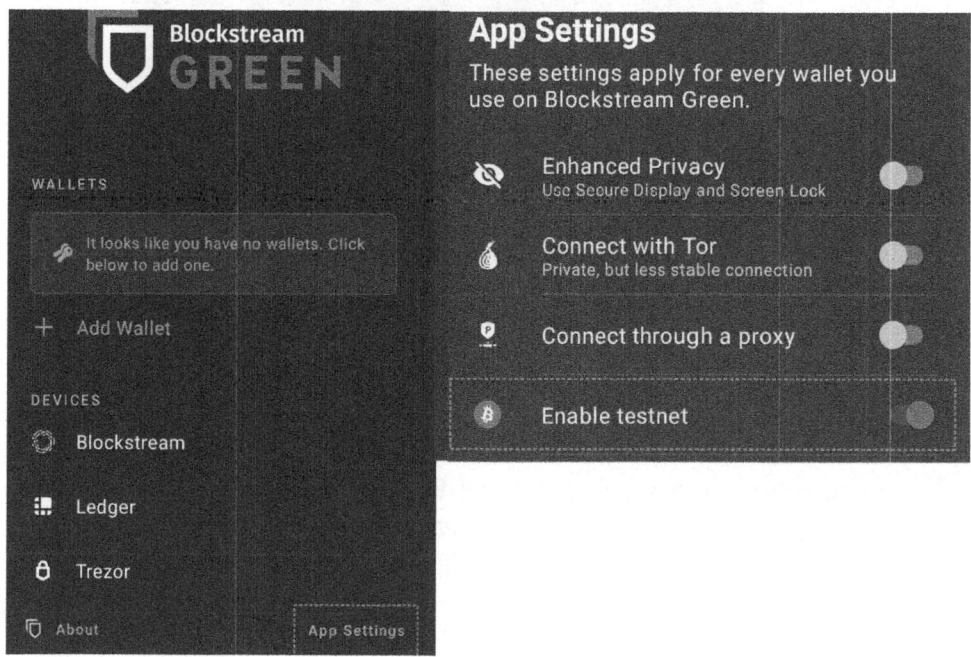

How to enable Bitcoin Testnet

---

57 tBTC are test bitcoins traded on the Bitcoin test network—the Testnet. tBTC have no monetary value.

Choose Your Network

Blockstream Green supports both Bitcoin and the Liquid Network. Don't worry, you can create another wallet for a different network at any time.

฿ Bitcoin

Bitcoin is the world's leading P2P cryptocurrency network. Select to send and receive bitcoin.

⌄ Additional Networks

฿ Testnet

Testnet network configuration screen.

Once you have created your new Testnet account, you can now press the "RECEIVE" button. To be able to send some tBTC, you will need to receive some first. To get some test bitcoins for this book, I used https://testnet-faucet.mempool.co.[58] So on Blockstream Green, once you press the "RECEIVE" button, you will receive a Testnet Bitcoin address. Use this address starting with "tb1" or "2" (legacy Testnet addresses start with the number 2) in the website mentioned above to send some Testnet coins to your Testnet Bitcoin address. If this website is down at the time you are reading this, simply type "bitcoin testnet faucet" in your search engine. Once the coins are sent to your address, you should see a screen that looks like this on your main account:

---

58 At the time of the publication of the English version of this book, testnet-faucet. mempool.co was not available. Try "bitcoin testnet faucet" in your favorite search engine. Or refer to this website: https://support.chainstack.com/hc/en-us/articles/900001638963-Bitcoin-testnet-faucets

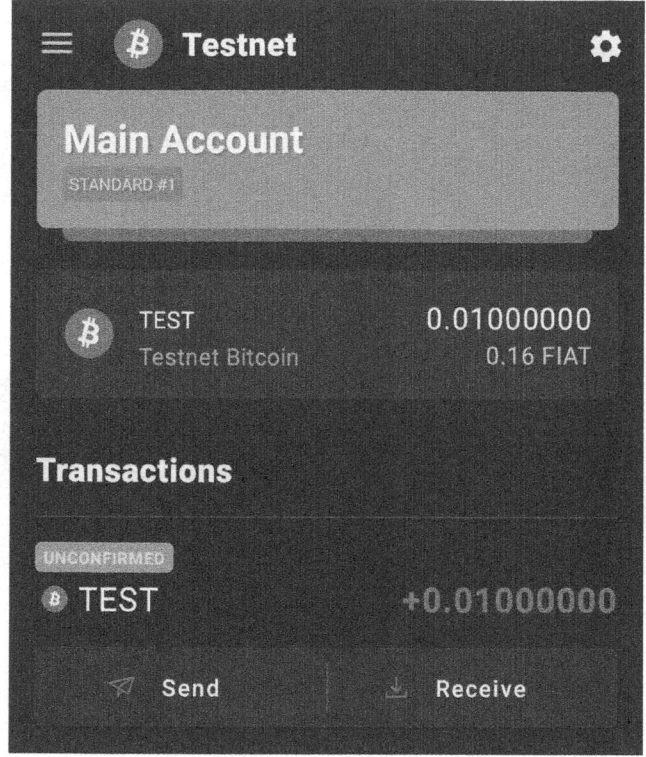

Testnet main account screen.

Notice the "Unconfirmed" tag on the transaction. Testnet works exactly like the real Bitcoin network. Blocks must be mined for your transaction to be included in the blockchain. While waiting for your transaction to be included in a block, you can go ahead and create another account in the wallet to which you are planning to send the coins. You can indeed send the coins to yourself. In the main Testnet account screen, click on the "Accounts" banner at the top of the screen.

Press "Add New Account." Choose the "legacy" account type. Give it a name, e.g. "Account #2." Once the account is added, select it and press the "Receive" button to generate an address, and copy it by tapping on the address. Return to your main account screen via the "Accounts" banner at the top and press the "Send" button. Paste the previously copied address into the "Send To" field and tap "Add Amount."

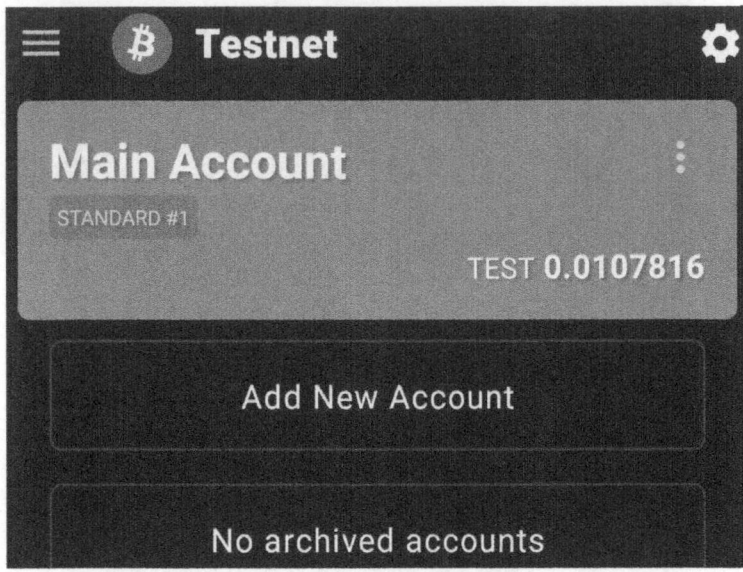
Adding a new account.

Specify how much you want to send. This must be less than your current balance as you will also need to add a transaction fee. Press "Verify," then "Drag to send."

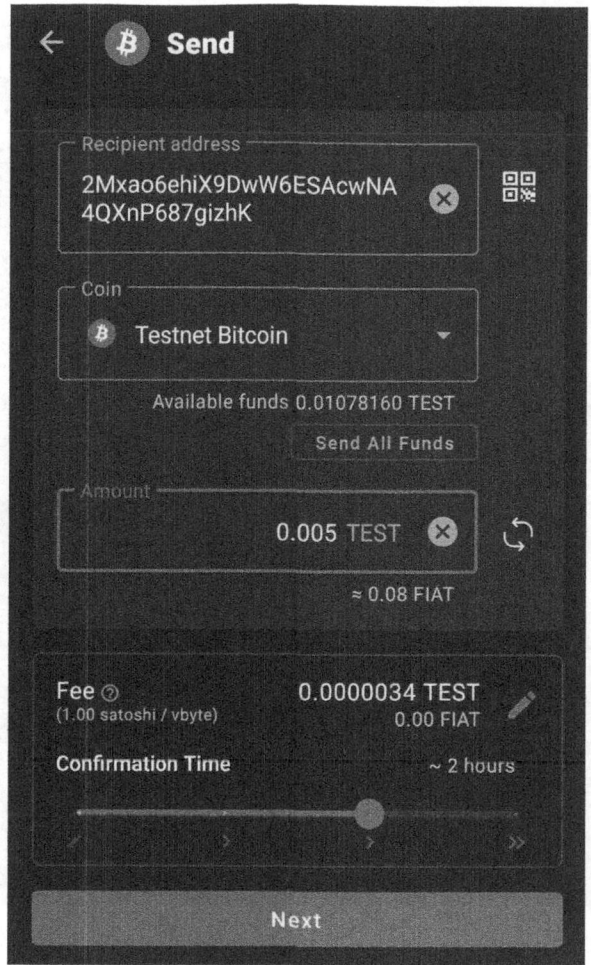

tBTC sending screen.

As you will see on your main account screen, your transaction will be confirmed as the blocks get mined. Congratulations! You've made your first Bitcoin transaction (on the Testnet).

It is recommended to return the tBTC to the faucet where you obtained them to allow others to use them in their experiments. An address is usually provided on the various faucet sites precisely for this purpose.

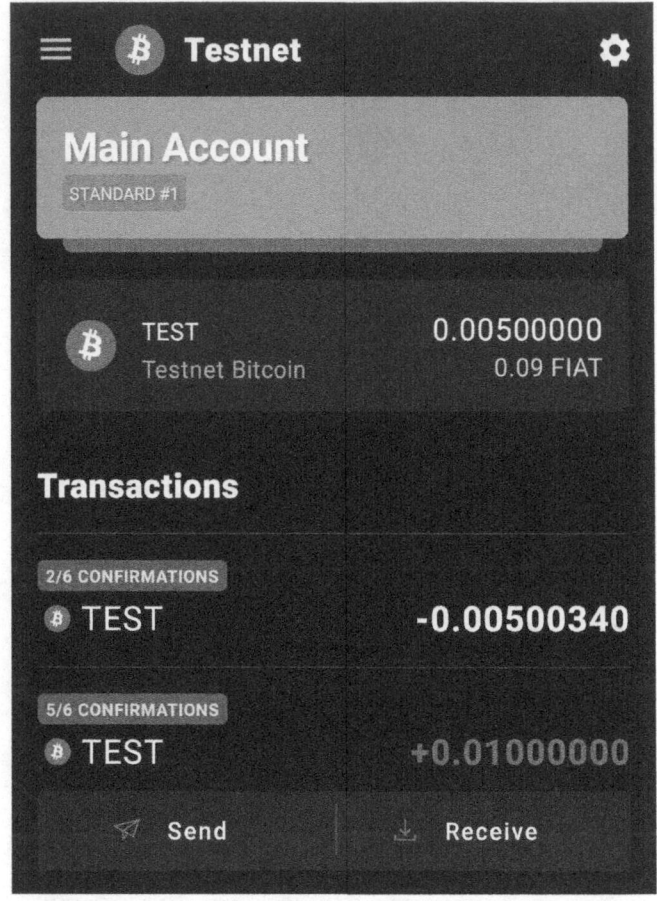

Example of a transaction received on the Testnet.

Number of confirmations

As you'll notice in the image shown above, once your transaction is included in the blockchain, it will say something along the lines of "X of 6 confirmations." This confirms that your transaction has been included in a block. When you receive two confirmations, it means that another block has been added on top of the block containing your transaction, and that your transaction has been confirmed by the network once again, and so on. Nowadays, six confirmations seem to be the norm for a transaction to be considered final. In the next chapter, we will unpack what the risks are in not waiting for this many confirmations before considering a transaction to be final.

USING YOUR OWN BITCOIN NODE

Why would you want to run a Bitcoin node? After all, your physical wallet already works just fine with the software provided by the company that makes it. So does the wallet on your smartphone.

As we saw earlier, your Bitcoin wallet is your gateway to the Bitcoin network. Your wallet is an interface that connects to a node on the network to query the blockchain or propagate a new transaction. By connecting to a node, your wallet reveals your public key to the node. Contrary to what the name suggests, your public key is not meant to be shared. We only share Bitcoin addresses with other users on the network; never our public key. Someone who knows one of your Bitcoin addresses can see the Bitcoin balance of that address and only that address—that's why you should always use a new address for each transaction. On the other hand, someone who has your public key can figure out all of your addresses and therefore know about all your assets tied to that public key.

That's why it's a good idea to run your own Bitcoin node and plug your wallet directly into it. Your wallet will still communicate your public key to the node, but since you own the node, your public key remains within your boundaries. Another reason you might want to consider using your own Bitcoin node is the possibility that a node you connect to may provide you with incorrect information: someone with bad intentions could give you an altered version of the Bitcoin blockchain. This is very unlikely to happen if you are using a wallet from an established company. Companies providing wallet services would have no interest in giving you an incorrect version of the blockchain for obvious reasons related to the reputation necessary to the very survival of the company. On the other hand, it is very possible—and this has happened to me personally—that for whatever reason, the infrastructure of said company is unavailable at the time you want to make a transaction or when you simply want to check your balance. At that point, you would have no choice but to wait for the situation to get better, or better yet, to connect to your own node!

Within Bitcoin's brief history, we currently find ourselves at a point in time when mining is undeniably an industrial operation requiring major investments in hardware as well as access to preferential energy rates. However, owning a Bitcoin node is an operation that anyone can do. "Node operator" is a term that might sound a bit too formal for what it is

© Dicoland

once you realize what it actually entails. To run a node, all a user needs is a computer and a hard drive with enough space to store the blockchain. At the time of writing, a 1TB hard drive is big enough to hold the current blockchain and accommodate all new blocks for at least another decade. Next, you need to download and install software, the most popular being Bitcoin Core. Of course, you need access to the Internet (or not—I'll come back to this in Chapter 9).

You'll probably agree with me that these requirements won't break the bank. This is without a doubt one of the main reasons why bitcoiners generally don't want to see an increase in block size, mainly to ensure that the cost of owning a node is kept as low as possible.

Running Your Own Bitcoin Node

At the time of writing, the official address for downloading Bitcoin Core is https://bitcoincore.org/en/download. It is absolutely imperative that you download Bitcoin Core's installer from a reliable website. At the time of writing, bitcoincore.org is the official website for downloading it. This may or may not change over time, so I highly recommend checking the official Bitcoin Core GitHub (https://github.com/bitcoin/bitcoin/releases) to make sure before proceeding with the download. Downloading Bitcoin Core from an unofficial website could have dire consequences for your Bitcoin adventure. In Appendix 2 of this book, I will also give you more details on the importance of verifying the authenticity of the code in the files you download.

Once you have downloaded the installation file (depending on your OS) you will need to run it and follow the on-screen instructions to complete the installation. At the end of the installation, please uncheck the "start Bitcoin Core" option, as we will be using the Testnet version of Bitcoin Core instead.

Configuring Bitcoin Core

To simplify your first steps in discovering the benefits of using your own Bitcoin node, I strongly suggest that you start your experimentation with the Testnet—so as not to risk your precious BTC—by using tBTC, the Testnet coins. They are worthless, so it isn't a big deal if you lose them.

The Testnet is Bitcoin's development network. Developers come here to test their creations.

Connecting Green Mobile Wallets to Your Node

Unfortunately, you need a little more than Bitcoin Core to connect your Green wallet to your node. Green wallet lets you connect to your own node through a personal Electrum Server. Installing and configuring an Electrum Server is beyond the scope of this book.

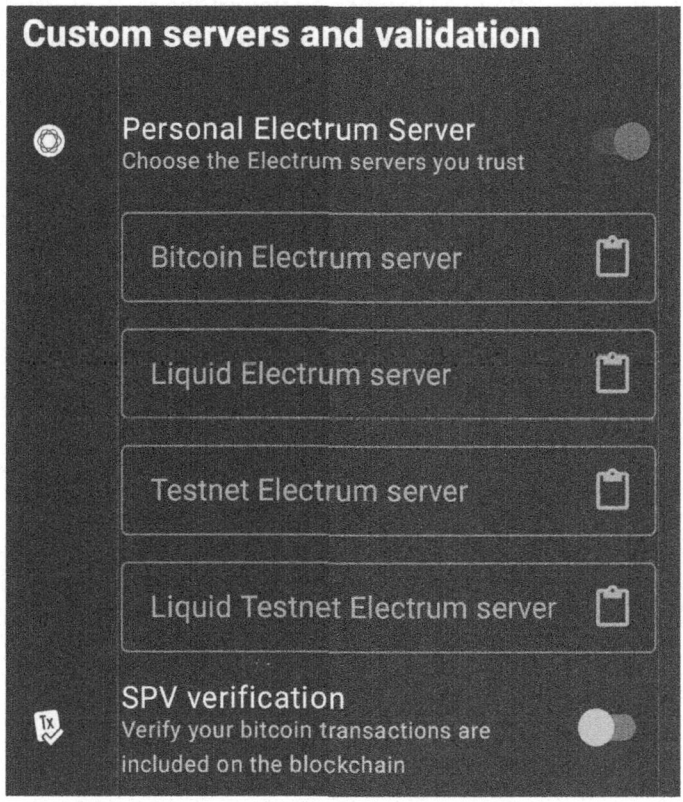

Blockstream Green personal server configuration screen.

Connecting your wallet to an Electrum Server is a big step in your journey in becoming a sovereign bitcoiner. Doing so will get you closer to adhering to the famous motto: "Don't trust, verify." Fortunately, some turnkey services let you deploy the tools you need to achieve this without too much hassle.

Turnkey services

Recently, new services have emerged that aim to make life easier for people wishing to run a Bitcoin node. Several products have come onto the market with a price ranging from naught to a few hundred dollars. Solutions that offer pre-configured hardware, including service and support, are available. Others offer DIY nodes with inexpensive hardware using the help of software tools that make it easy to deploy and install the various modules. Personally, I chose the paid version of MyNodeBTC, available at https://mynodebtc.com/. It is possible to install their product on a Raspberry Pi-type mini-computer. This solution integrates a multitude of products already configured to work on your node, such as wallet servers, blockchain visualization tools, an anonymized connection through Tor, the BTCPay Server application, Electrum Server and much more. Umbrel offers the same type of services and a lot of other self-hosting cloud apps. You can find out more about Umbrel at: https://umbrel.com.

Part III
BITCOIN'S FUTURE

CHAPTER 8.
BITCOIN'S OPPONENTS

"As long as a majority of CPU power is controlled by nodes that are not cooperating to attack the network, they'll generate the longest chain and outpace attackers."

—Satoshi Nakamoto

L et's turn to the security aspect of Bitcoin. You might be wondering if Bitcoin could be hacked; or what would happen if a government or other governmental agency were to hack Bitcoin. What if a government or a malicious group took control, or simply blocked Internet traffic? And what would happen if a government decided to make Bitcoin outright illegal? This chapter will focus on describing Bitcoin's current and potential adversaries as well as other threatening risks. However, let me reassure you right now: Bitcoin is "antifragile."[59]

51% ATTACKS

Bitcoin is a completely decentralized network with no controlling authority. It's the network's consensus mechanism that dictates the status of transactions to all participants: Does a given transaction exist or does

---

59 In reference to Nassim Nicholas Taleb's book, *Antifragile: Things That Gain From Disorder.*

it not exist? Has the balance of an existing transaction been spent or not? Reality is dictated by the blockchain. This is how a completely decentralized consensus system can exist.

To make these threats more tangible, let's see how we could potentially force the network to accept our reality as *the* reality. Because yes, there is a way to force Bitcoin into accepting a different version of reality. It's a fairly widely known fact in the world of blockchains, and it's what we call a "51% attack." Basically, if someone were to control more than half of the network's power, he could impose his own version of reality upon the network. The attacker may be motivated either by a desire to double-spend or to simply undermine the blockchain. He would not be able to steal coins that already belong to someone else, nor would he be able to create new coins or give himself a bigger block subsidy. As we have covered previously, the Bitcoin network's validation rules—imposed by the nodes—prevent miners, whether honest or not, from changing the rules of the game.

DOUBLE-SPENDING

Let's imagine a malicious individual who shows up at a luxury car dealership that accepts Bitcoin as a form of payment. The individual in question chooses a beautiful car, worth $500,000. He pulls out his phone and sends the equivalent of that amount in BTC to the Bitcoin address provided by the seller. At the same time, using another phone, he signals his accomplice to launch a 51% attack on the network before driving away in his new car. Meanwhile, on the Bitcoin network, the mining devices controlled by the thief are busy winning the race to mine the next block. Since he controls the majority of the network, he manages to find the block before the other miners. The thief had previously prepared a transaction that sends the same coins as those that were supposed to pay for the car, to an address that belongs to him. Of course, when the thief's mining device broadcasts the block on the network, the "fraudulent" transaction will appear before the one intended for the seller, making the latter invalid. In the end, the thief will have left the car dealership with a beautiful new car, without having spent the equivalent of its price, i.e. $500,000 in bitcoins.

This example illustrates the risk of a double-spend attack, keeping in mind however that the cost of setting up such an operation is far from trivial, and its modalities are particularly complex due to the mining power required to achieve it.

CHAIN REORGANIZATION

It is impossible to steal someone's coins without owning the private keys required to spend them. In the car salesman example above, the thief diverted his own coins because he owned the private keys. In his attack, he created a separate transaction, sending the funds to his address instead of the seller's, and made sure that this malicious transaction had priority over the other one on the blockchain. You can't steal bitcoins without owning the private keys that control them. However, an attacker could potentially deprive you of your bitcoins by deleting and overwriting the transaction in which the coins were originally sent to you. From the blockchain's perspective, you would never have received those coins in the first place. In other words, you can't be robbed of your bitcoins, but you could be deprived of them. A malicious person with more than half the hash power on the network could very well mine an empty chain for three months and suddenly decide to release it onto the network. If this chain has more Proof-of-Work (PoW) than the current chain, the nodes would have no choice but to accept the "fraudulent" chain as the new chain, and thus as the new reality. This would be equivalent to a Denial-of-Service attack, the goal being to prevent users from using the Bitcoin network.

The Cost of a 51% Attack

All this of course seems quite worrying. How can we be sure that a group or a state isn't, at this very moment, preparing or executing such an attack on the network? I will now lay out the enormous costs of carrying out such an attack, instead of simply telling you that "it's almost impossible since it would be too expensive," as we often read on this subject. We're actually going to calculate that cost. Don't trust, verify!

When we briefly discussed the possibility of creating a list of all possible Bitcoin private keys, we concluded that it was impossible, simply because the universe wouldn't even be big enough to record them all. Similarly, a 51% attack on the Bitcoin network is highly unlikely, since an attack of this magnitude would require a phenomenal amount of energy. As long as the Bitcoin network remains as strong as it is, it is very unlikely that anyone would have access to that much power. But don't just take my word for it; let's do the math together.

The power of the Bitcoin network is calculated using the number of hashes generated per second, or H/s. A hash is simply the result of a hash function. A hash function accepts any data as its input, and then produces an alphanumeric sequence with a predefined size that "summarizes" the input. For example, if I provide the text "Bitcoin: Everything You Need to Know" to the Bitcoin hash function, I get the following hash:

a5da69491ab5db8f3784fcfa0c500450a7ad06553f-3b3e556428b2613b1da5ce

The current hash rate at the time of writing (2020)[60] is estimated to be at 120 million TH/s. This is just an estimate based on a calculation involving the number of blocks mined over a certain timeframe with the network's current difficulty level. 120 million TH/s is equivalent to generating 120 quintillion hashes per second—that's 120 followed by 15 zeros.

Necessary Materials

The first step in measuring the cost to carry out a 51% attack would be to calculate the value of the necessary equipment. We will count how many devices Bitmain[61] would need to provide us with in order to outperform the network's current hash power.

A mining device is simply a kind of computer containing ultra-specialized chips that perform hashing operations. Bitmain's Antminer S19[62] offers a hash rate of 95 TH/s and sells for 1,785 USD. This means that you would need to purchase 1,263,158 Antminer S19 devices to surpass the current network power. This would cost a whopping 2,254,737,030 USD. I would also add that it simply isn't possible to get hundreds of thousands of devices like that in one go. The suppliers of mining devices have finite production capabilities. It is obvious that if one group decided to take

---

60 It has more than doubled since then, reaching 260 million TH/s in 2022.

61 https://www.bitmain.com

62 https://shop.bitmain.com/product/detail?pid=00020200611225624412AP
vsi9V70691

over the entire global production of mining devices, it would immediately attract the attention of many in the industry.

Energy Costs

Now that we know how much we would need to invest in hardware to outperform the current Bitcoin network, let's look at the amount of energy that would be needed to carry out the attack. Each of these devices uses 3,250 watts of power, thus consuming 3.25 kilowatt-hours (kWh) per hour. Quebec has the cheapest energy in North America.[63] The residential rate is set at just over 0.09 CAD per kWh, which is equivalent to about 0.07 USD at the time of writing.

Therefore, 1,263,158 devices * 3.25 kWh * 0.07 USD = 287,368 USD per hour.

Energy Access

With 1,263,158 appliances consuming 3.25 kWh per hour each, our network of bad actors would need 4,105,264 kWh or 4.1 gigawatt-hours or GWh (Yes! Gigawatts, like the 1.21 GW mentioned in "Back to the Future"). To compare this energy expenditure with e.g. that of a country, it must be calculated over a year. 4.1 GWh multiplied by 8,760 hours (the number of hours in a year) gives us 36.9 terawatt-hours or TWh. This is equivalent to the total electricity consumption of a small country. In Quebec, for instance, 190 TWh are expected to be consumed in 2020.[64] In 2011, the annual consumption of the city of Montreal reached 29.9 TWh.[65] My intention isn't at all to portray myself as an expert in matters of energy supply, but my personal guess would be that negotiating a contract for an energy supply that could potentially be used by a world-class metropolis is likely not a trivial task to undertake. Even the Quebec government, armed with its state-owned Hydro-Québec, which has an energy surplus

---

63 https://www.hydroquebec.com/residential/customer-space/rates/

64 https://www.journaldemontreal.com/2019/11/03/hydro-quebec-sattend-a-epuis-er-son-energie-disponible-en-2026

65 http://ville.montreal.qc.ca/portal/page?_pageid=6897,67889708&_dad=portal&_schema=PORTAL

of 18 TWh,[66] would not be able to launch an attack on Bitcoin. To do so, Hydro-Québec would have to offload massive amounts of energy from its distribution network

Supply Chains

Furthermore, even if we were able to access all that energy, we must also realize that the Bitcoin network's ability to grow is limited by the production rate of the devices that make up the network. You can't simply make more than a million computers appear out of thin air. There is a whole supply chain underlying the production of electronic equipment. Its production capacity is finite and planned months or even years in advance. In my opinion, it would be impossible to assemble all the necessary equipment fast enough to implement a 51% attack. In summary, even if a group had access to enough capital to acquire the equipment required to launch this kind of attack, it is unlikely that they would be able to gather all the equipment anyway, for the reasons mentioned above.

HASH POWER CENTRALIZATION

There is, however, another way to control more than half of the network's hash power. Someone who controls a sufficient number of devices, giving them access to more than half of the network's hash power, would probably be able to carry out a 51% attack. That's why it's important for there to be a minimum level of decentralization in the Bitcoin mining industry. If one group held more than half of the hash power, it would put the entire network at risk—this would be true even if the group were honest, as their equipment could be targeted by malicious hackers. In reality, because the hash power is relatively well distributed with multiple mining groups scattered throughout the globe, this type of attack would require an extraordinary level of coordination that seems highly unlikely.

The main point to keep in mind is that all this effort would only result in a few double-spending attacks in the end. If they had that much power in their hands, pirates would be better off mining and cashing in on the block subsidies instead. Especially given that a merchant only has to wait

---

66 https://www.journaldequebec.com/2019/10/04/hydro-quebec-perd-des-ventes-dun-milliard-par-annee

for a certain number of confirmations to avoid the risk of a double-spend attack. Usually, six confirmations are enough, i.e. one hour. However, a car dealer, especially a luxury car dealer, could wait 24 hours: in order to carry out an attack on the last 144 mined blocks (equivalent to 24 hours), it would cost nearly 7 million USD. Not very profitable when stealing a $500,000 car. The waiting time required can be adjusted according to the value of the purchase. Referring back to our chain reorganization attack in which a hacker would want to rewrite three months of the blockchain, it would cost them over 620 million USD in energy expenditure to catch up and overtake the current chain.

ENERGY FOOTPRINT

Many of Bitcoin's detractors often raise the thorny issue regarding the large energy expenditure that is so essential to the security of the Bitcoin network. It is thanks to the large energy expenditure involved in Proof-of-Work that the Bitcoin network is so secure. I sometimes hear people complain that Bitcoin "wastes" a lot of energy. There is no doubt that Bitcoin uses a lot of energy, but is that energy wasted? Absolutely not. The Bitcoin network doesn't spend energy unnecessarily, because it provides a service. Does the global gold industry waste energy? Do the security systems of all the world's financial institutions waste energy? Of course not! When our level of technology improves and our quality of life increases, this always comes with an increase in energy expenditure. Bitcoin is no different.

VULNERABILITIES

This is probably the most insidious risk. Imagine a technical problem that breaks Bitcoin and causes its price to plummet. This happened in 2010: a simple anomaly in the code at the time allowed a user to create 184 billion bitcoins. This problem was identified and quickly corrected. This is why Bitcoin's code must be kept simple. Today, Bitcoin is being developed by a team of volunteers and seasoned developers. It is no longer a technological experiment like it was in 2009–2010. There is no doubt in my mind that today, with all the effort put into quality assurance, the chances of such vulnerabilities being deployed in production are slim.

Moreover, since Bitcoin is a completely decentralized network and no one is forced to run the latest version proposed by the developers, a bug introduced in a recent version would not affect nodes running an earlier version of the software.

OTHER CRYPTOCURRENCIES

During your first days learning about Bitcoin, you will no doubt hear or read that Bitcoin is an outdated technology, that you should actually be interested in the blockchain rather than Bitcoin, that innovation lies elsewhere, and that Bitcoin is too limited anyway—too slow, or not anonymous enough. You'll quickly notice that those who tell you this garbage always have something that they want to sell you. It almost always involves a "revolutionary" token that solves all of Bitcoin's problems in one fell swoop, pushing the blockchain "much further," and which, of course, will make you fabulously rich for investing in it. And to top it all off, these people invariably want to sell you these so-called "revolutionary tokens" in exchange for your "boring old bitcoins," because "it's good to diversify." Allow me to express my doubts... That said, don't take my word for it. I invite the skeptics to find out for themselves why such "revolutionary" projects exist.

HARD FORKS

Bitcoin gave us digital scarcity, a phenomenon that did not exist before its invention. For the first time ever, it became possible for a person to purchase a digital object, and to be certain that he or she is the only one in the universe to own it. That's what the discovery of Bitcoin provided us with.

To understand how hard forks work, I will offer an analogy using a fictional magic jar. This will help you understand one of Bitcoin's immutable rules regarding the process of validating transactions, as well as the consequences of violating this rule.

Say you have a blue marble and you put it in a jar full of marbles. The marbles all have different colors, but no other marble has the same blue color as yours. This marble jar is also magical: it cannot contain two marbles of the same color. If you add a marble whose color already exists inside the jar, a new jar magically appears out of thin air. The marble that was excluded from the first jar will be found all alone in the second jar. Thanks to this rule, you can be sure that your blue marble is the only one of its color in the first jar. You can even verify it.

This is exactly what happens with Bitcoin's protocol. When you don't follow the protocol's rules, you are simply ejected from the network. Your blue marble will automatically end up in a new jar (the second jar) as soon as you try to break the rules set by the first magic jar. If you decide to change the software code running on your Bitcoin node to reward a miner with, say, 1,000 coins per block instead of 6.25—as stipulated by the current emission schedule—then that block will be instantly rejected by the other nodes on the network. You could then decide to add another 100 nodes running this modified code to the network. These 100 nodes would now accept your block containing your 1,000 fraudulent coins, but since they would be the only nodes to accept your block, you would end up on another blockchain, i.e. a hard fork. Your 1,000 fraudulent coins would exist, but they would be worthless to users of the real Bitcoin network. You wouldn't be able to trade them on the nodes running the original protocol's code (equivalent to the first magic jar in our analogy). You would effectively be kicked off the network. You would have your separate "new jar" containing your single lonely little blue marble. You would finally realize that your marble (or forked bitcoin) is worthless as it does not exist in the "first jar," where the marbles (or real bitcoins) have actual value.

Such hard forks give rise to new cryptocurrencies. Bitcoin Cash (BCH), created in 2017, is the first example of a Bitcoin hard fork. It occurred because a fringe group in the Bitcoin community thought that the block size was too small. In the absence of consensus, nodes preferring to operate with an increased block size joined the BCH fork, creating a new blockchain as well as a new cryptocurrency. There have been dozens of other such hard forks, most of which have become virtually worthless.

The main problem with these Bitcoin hard forks is that once these blockchains go their own way, they are no longer protected by the main chain's incredible hash power. Bitcoin Cash, for example, only enjoys about 2–3% of Bitcoin's hash rate at the time of writing. Some advocates of this cryptocurrency claim that this is more than enough to keep the network safe, but even if this were true, it would only be so if Bitcoin

Cash used a different hash algorithm. That's because, at any time, someone with access to 1–2% of Bitcoin's hash rate could redirect it to the Bitcoin Cash blockchain and perform a double-spend or Denial-of-Service attack. When it comes to Bitcoin's hash algorithm, SHA-256, the only chain that is safe is the Bitcoin chain. All other blockchains could be attacked at any time with a tiny fraction of the power used by the Bitcoin network.

Another important problem with these hard forks, in my opinion, is the inevitable centralization that comes with them: there is always an individual, a group, or a foundation behind the various Bitcoin hard forks and other blockchain projects. This fact alone renders these projects less decentralized than Bitcoin. Nobody knows who Bitcoin's inventor really is. The entity or group known as Satoshi Nakamoto is not the one pulling Bitcoin's strings. Bitcoin is truly decentralized, unlike any other blockchain or cryptocurrency that has been created since. And even if the identity of Satoshi Nakamoto were to become known, he/she/they would not suddenly become the "CEO" of Bitcoin. Bitcoin does not have a CEO, nor will it ever have one, and that is precisely what distinguishes Bitcoin from all other cryptocurrencies.

BITCOIN COPYCATS

Many people see fit to copy Bitcoin's code, tweaking its parameters for a wide variety of reasons, stemming from thinking that Bitcoin isn't fast enough, or that there aren't enough coins, or perhaps that the color of the logo is too orange. Thus, Bitcoin copycats abound. Unfortunately (or rather, fortunately), all the qualities that make Bitcoin unique cannot simply be recreated by copying or "improving" its code. Bitcoin's uniqueness stems from its network's hash power and the creator's anonymity. My only advice is that you should not pay attention to this kind of nonsense.

SMART CONTRACT PLATFORMS

There are other forms of cryptocurrencies that are potentially more meaningful than simple copies of Bitcoin. This is the case with smart contract platforms like Ethereum, which indeed offer much more than a simple change in a few code parameters, or the logo being a different color. These platforms use the blockchain's characteristics to produce "uncensorable" pieces of code that allow the creation of all sorts of so-called "decentralized" financial services.

Some supporters of these platforms even assure us that their project will most certainly surpass Bitcoin in terms of market capitalization. Personally, I doubt it. But even if this were to happen, one should not forget that these platforms were created with an entirely different purpose in mind than what Bitcoin aims to achieve. Ethereum cannot compete with Bitcoin on the hard money front, since its monetary policy can be changed. Also, it should be kept in mind that the value of these tokens lies in the usefulness of their platform as a system for smart contracts. If one of these platforms were to suffer a major flaw or simply get overtaken by a competitor, the value of their token would inevitably suffer. Thus, Bitcoin and these smart contract platforms are not in the same market. On the one hand, we have Bitcoin, which is essentially digital cash. On the other hand, we have these utility tokens, which would be more comparable to consumer goods, because their use case is to basically allow you to take advantage of the services offered by these systems. They have value as long as their platform is useful. As for Bitcoin, as long as its (simpler) code remains stable, and as long as there is a demand for an alternative monetary system that is resistant to censorship, it will continue to enjoy the benefits of being in demand, assuring it a certain value.

THE STATE

What would prevent a state from declaring the possession of bitcoins as illegal? This is a plausible scenario. The US government did this to its population with gold back in 1933.[67] Since the US dollar is the world's reserve currency, there is constant demand for it. This gives the United States an invaluable privilege. Thanks to this constant demand for the greenback, Americans can afford to run deficits and to *make the money printer go brrr,* as the saying goes, without having to worry too much

---

67 In 1933, the US government forced all American citizens to "convert" their gold coins and bars into US dollars, and outright declared the possession of gold as a form of currency as illegal. The ban was not lifted until 1974.

about a sharp devaluation of their currency. This state of affairs has been referred to by the French Minister of Finance in the 1960s—and more famously, albeit later, by Charles de Gaulle—as the US' "exorbitant privilege." So it is quite possible that the US government will not go down without a fight if Bitcoin ever threatens the US dollar's hegemony.

Meanwhile, Bitcoin continues its slow progress in terms of legal compliance and recognition. In fact, on July 22, 2020, the OCC (Office of the Comptroller of the Currency) in the United States announced that banks will now be able to act as cryptocurrency depositories. Hopefully, this slow progress will reach a point of no return. It will indeed be more complicated to ban Bitcoin once commercial banks have invested in developing all sorts of Bitcoin-based products and commercial offerings.

In any case, even if a state were to ban Bitcoin, Bitcoin remains permissionless. Remember Libra? In 2019, when this new cryptocurrency was announced, the US government was quick to summon its instigators before a committee of the House of Representatives.[68] The project has since been put on hold until the regulatory landscape becomes clearer. Bitcoin, on the other hand, has no CEO or "instigators." Bitcoin's CEO cannot be called before a congressional committee. And even if a state were to block the Internet, Bitcoin could continue to operate on another network. Blockstream already allows the Bitcoin blockchain to be downloaded directly from space via its Blockstream Satellite service. Furthermore, some hackers are working on mesh network technologies that will offer an alternative to the Internet. And we haven't even talked about the Starlink network yet. Imagine a country that decides to "ban the Internet": its inhabitants could simply fall back on a satellite Internet provider such as Starlink to bypass this measure.

CENSORSHIP AND REGULATORY CAPTURE

The battle will likely be fought on both fronts: transaction censorship as well as regulation. We see this happening right now with the (failed) attempt by the mining company Marathon to create blocks that comply with the Office of Foreign Assets Control (OFAC) regulations, or with the recent arrest of the developer of an open-source tool related to privacy.

---

68 https://www.theguardian.com/technology/2019/oct/23/mark-zuckerberg-congress-testimony-libra-facebook

We can also mention here the growing interest of the SEC in the United States for the Ethereum platform, especially in connection with the staking of tokens in exchange for a return. The SEC even insinuates that the entire network (Ethereum) could now be placed under its jurisdiction.

We can also mention the efforts of Greenpeace, which is stepping up its "Change the Code. Not the Climate."[69] campaign, launched in March 2022; they are urging the major financial institutions that have recently started to embrace Bitcoin to pressure its community into changing Bitcoin's consensus mechanism to one that is more "energy efficient." Finally, it is difficult to ignore the European Parliament's desire to legislate a ban on "unhosted wallets," i.e. wallets that are not hosted by a trusted third party.

You will certainly understand that this initiative makes no sense for a system whose entire raison d'être is precisely to allow exchanges of digital value to occur WITHOUT the need to trust a third party.

---

69 https://www.greenpeace.org/usa/news/change-the-code-not-the-climate-green-peace-usa-ewg-others-launch-campaign-to-push-bitcoin-to-reduce-climate-pollu-tion/

© Dicoland

CHAPTER 9.
BITCOIN'S FUTURE

I'm sure that in 20 years there will either be very large transaction volume or no volume.

—Satoshi Nakomoto

Sometimes, I feel like I'm living in a movie. I'm writing a book about Bitcoin during a global pandemic in which governments are shutting down their economies and turning to quantitative easing[70] to try to repair the damage that they caused. We are in the midst of an unprecedented global, monetary, social and political experiment: a system based on perpetual growth, fueled by debt. In his book *The Price of Tomorrow,* Jeff Booth writes that between the year 2000 and the end of 2018, the value of the global economy grew from $33.5 trillion to about $80 trillion. He also reports that during the same period, global debt increased from $62 trillion to $247 trillion. Thus, to generate $46 trillion in growth, there was a $185 trillion cost in debt. Booth argues that to generate an additional $46 trillion in growth, we would now need to more than double this $185 trillion in debt.[71]

The morning I sat down to begin writing this chapter, I came across a Bloomberg.com article on my Twitter feed. This article claimed that some Fed officials are beginning to invoke the possibility of overshooting their

---

[70] Quantitative easing is a monetary policy action whereby a central bank purchases government bonds during exceptional economic circumstances, such as economic crises.

[71] Jeff Booth, *The Price of Tomorrow,* 2020.

inflation target.[72] Here's another one: the day I finished writing the section on Zimbabwe, I learned that the country is back to printing money and resurrecting an inflationary spiral.[73] And that's not counting the situation in Lebanon—as I type this, there is a report on Radio-Canada that tries to explain the circumstances that led to their hyperinflation.[74] In another report, a civil servant in Beirut tells us that her monthly salary has dropped from the equivalent of $1,800 per month to $400 in the space of six months.[75] One more: on July 25, 2020, The Economist headlined: "Free money: When government spending knows no limits."[76] On September 29, 2022, while editing this section for the English version of this book, the Financial Times headlines: "Bank of England unleashes £65bn bid to avert crisis in debt markets." A headline reminiscent of the famous Times headline inscribed forever, by Satoshi himself, on Bitcoin's genesis block.

The more one looks into this subject, the more one wonders about the sustainability of such a system. Remember that this monstrous accumulation of debt is only possible because central banks have the power to print money out of thin air, and commercial banks can lend any one dollar multiple times. It was not possible to accumulate so much debt under the gold standard. It would be even less possible under a Bitcoin standard.

You know how in disaster movies, you often hear the media in the background dramatically describing the catastrophic situation that's going on? Well, that's what my life felt like in 2020. A long movie in which the subject I'm writing about is described to me every day, in the background, on my radio or Twitter feed. Some of the content of this book was written in real-time while I received relevant information directly related to what I was writing.

Don't worry, I won't bring back the eternal philosophical question of whether human beings are born with free will or whether our destiny is

72 https://www.bloomberg.com/opinion/articles/2020-07-17/the-fed-is-setting-the-stage-for-a-major- policy-change

73 https://www.cnbc.com/2020/07/17/zimbabwe-could-be-headed-for-political-up-heaval-as-econo- mic-health-crises-spiral.html

74 Lebanon's descent into hell https://ici.radio-canada.ca/premiere/emissions/de-sautels-le-dimanche/segments/entrevue/189349/crise-economique-liban-karim-emile-bitar

75 https://ici.radio-canada.ca/premiere/emissions/desautels-le-dimanche/epi-sodes/481720/rattrapage-du-dimanche-20-septembre-2020/9

76 https://www.economist.com/weeklyedition/2020-07-25

written in advance. These situations are of course pure happenstance, or at least a remarkable proof of how relevant and anchored in the present this subject really is. We already find ourselves at the end of the book... where I will now start laying out what the future holds for Bitcoin.

THE FUTURE OF BANKING

I am far from being an advocate of the anti-bank rhetoric preached by many bitcoiners. In my opinion, commercial banks provide services that meet their customers' demands. The problem with the current banking system does not lie in the commercial banks, but rather in the central banks. Let's imagine for a moment that commercial banks are operating on the Bitcoin network. In the fiat world, if you want to leave the banking system, you either have to show up in person with bags to withdraw your cash assets (assuming the bank accepts) or transfer your funds electronically to another bank—which means you're not actually leaving the banking system. You cannot transfer your electronically held cash funds to your own system unless you yourself are a bank.

BEING YOUR OWN BANK

This is precisely what Bitcoin allows you to do. One of the reasons why banks are able to maintain the fractional reserve banking system is that your funds are literally trapped in this system. Banks are betting on the fact that the risk of depositors withdrawing all their funds at the same time is very low, allowing them to lend the same dollar multiple times.

Under a Bitcoin-based system, there would be no physical barrier to bank runs. Depositors would not have to wait in line to get their cash, and withdrawals would not be limited by the amount of physical cash a local bank branch has in stock. A bank's customers could, at any time and for any reason, transfer their funds electronically, to their own Bitcoin addresses, in their own wallets, linked to their own Bitcoin nodes. Would this risk of mass withdrawals force banks to manage their capitalization differently? This remains to be seen. In any case, the use of Bitcoin in the current banking system would effectively end the banks' monopoly on the electronic custody of money (and it could very well happen faster than one might think).[77] As we have seen, the Office of the Comptroller of the Currency (OCC) announced in July 2020 that US banks will be able to hold crypto assets for their customers.[78] What's more, in January 2021, the same OCC issued a memo mentioning the use of cryptocurrencies as a settlement infrastructure between banks.[79]

Bitcoin gives you a choice. If you want to keep your assets at a bank that you already trust, you can. If that trust simply breaks down or if something more serious happens, you may be able to retrieve those assets electronically (if you are fast enough), and then you can just be your own bank and assume the risks and rewards.

BITCOIN AS A GLOBAL RESERVE CURRENCY

I think this would be the ultimate dream for every bitcoiner: a Bitcoin standard, i.e. the use of Bitcoin as a reserve currency in the world's central banks. This would effectively sound the death knell for state currencies, and more importantly, it would end the "exorbitant privilege" enjoyed by the United States, fixing the historical mistake[80] that led to US hegemony. Bitcoin took its first baby steps on its path towards becoming a global reserve currency in 2021, when El Salvador officially declared it as legal tender.

WALL STREET

Although Bitcoin is often portrayed by the mainstream media as a scam or a tool used by criminals, it seems that this does not stop people on Wall Street from taking an interest in it. In an article published on Medium,[81] Mark Helfman points out that several large firms are already expressing in-

---

77 https://www.economist.com/weeklyedition/2020-07-25

78 Federally Chartered Banks and Thrifts May Provide Custody Services For Crypto Assets →https://www.occ.gov/news-issuances/news-releases/2020/nr-occ-2020-98.html

79 Federally Chartered Banks and Thrifts May Participate in Independent Node Verification Networks and Use Stablecoins for Payment Activities → https://www.occ.gov/news-issuances/ news-releases/2021/nr-occ-2021-2.html

80 Jacques Rueff, *Le péché Monétaire de L'Occident*, Paris 1971.

81 https://medium.com/swlh/goldman-sachs-can-say-whatever-it-wants-wall-street-is-still-buying-your-bitcoin-2f859a432b0d

terest in cryptocurrencies, namely JP Morgan, State Street, Fidelity, and TD Ameritrade. His article cites Grayscale, a firm that allegedly bought 150% of all bitcoins mined in 2020 until the article was published in late May.

At the other end of the spectrum, a subsidiary of Goldman Sachs reportedly announced in a late May paper that Bitcoin is not a suitable investment for its clients. Mark Helfman summarizes Goldman Sachs' position as follows: "The stuff we sell is good. The stuff we don't sell is not good." You may be surprised to hear me say this, but I have to say that I agree with them. First, I think I've made it very clear that I don't see Bitcoin as an investment, but rather as an alternative to state currencies. That said, those who bet on Bitcoin now may be greatly rewarded in the future.

The problem for Wall Street firms that won't adopt Bitcoin is the following: what happens when some of their clients want to invest, say, 1% of their portfolio in Bitcoin? One example is Paul Tudor, whose Tudor BVI fund holds a few percent in Bitcoin, much like an inflation insurance policy.[82]

THE USE OF SURPLUS ENERGY

In the previous chapter, we talked about Bitcoin's energy consumption. Here, I'd like to make an argument regarding the grid's energy footprint. Let's take the example of Hydro-Québec, the government corporation responsible for the production, transmission, and distribution of electricity in Quebec. Hydro-Québec's total electricity generation capacity is not based on the average Québécois' energy usage over a year, but on an estimate of the total energy required to meet peak demand. The Crown Corporation's total capacity is therefore much higher than the average consumption of its distribution network. Moreover, by its own admission, Hydro-Québec currently has an energy surplus of about 18 TWh in 2020. Since most of this surplus comes from wind and hydroelectricity, this energy is readily available and does not require the combustion of fuel.

Let's now have fun calculating how many bitcoins Hydro-Québec could potentially obtain with its 2020 surplus. For this exercise, let's take the same device we used in one of our previous examples, the Antminer S19 from Bitmain. Each of these devices uses 3,250 watts of energy, thus con-

82 https://www.bloomberg.com/news/articles/2020-05-07/paul-tudor-jones-buys-bitcoin-says-he-s-reminded-of-gold-in-70s

suming 3.25 kWh per hour.[83] An annual surplus of 18 TWh could power 632,244 miners. Each of these devices costs 1,785 USD. The investment poured into equipment would therefore amount to at least 1 billion USD (to which we would of course need to add a host of other costs, but for this exercise, we will keep our calculations as simple as possible).

What would the revenue potential be for such a venture? For the current period spanning from 2020 to 2024, the Bitcoin network's block subsidy is at 6.25 BTC per block. With a block mined every 10 minutes on average, and assuming each bitcoin priced at an average of 10,000 USD, the potential value of the block subsidies paid to miners in one year can be estimated at nearly 3.3 billion USD. The hash power of the current network is estimated at 120,000,000 TH/s. Since our hypothetical 632,244 devices alone would produce more than 60,000,000 TH/s, we would suddenly have about 33% of the total hash power of the network, thus potentially around 33% of the bitcoins obtained through block subsidies. With 328,500 bitcoins to be distributed per year over the next four years, we could therefore generate 109,500 bitcoins per year using Hydro-Québec's surplus. Keep in mind that this calculation only takes into account Hydro-Québec's surplus. We haven't even included their unused capacity during off-peak periods.

That is, with its annual surplus of 18 TWh and an investment of around 1 billion USD, Hydro-Québec could potentially generate the equivalent of 109,500 bitcoins worth over 1 billion USD[84] every single year. And in 2018, Hydro-Québec was forced to spill the equivalent of 10 TWh while its reservoirs were overflowing in northern Quebec.[85] All of this energy could have generated more than 500 million CAD in BTC. Speaking of waste, in my opinion, this is the real waste. Here's my proposal: build bitcoin mining plants near hydroelectricity companies' distribution networks and exploit their unused energy production during consumption lows to generate bitcoins. Of course, the opportunity to open these mining plants should be offered to private entrepreneurs. Hydro-Québec could attract them with preferential rates, much like it already does with other industries like aluminum smelters for example. On June 5, 2019, Hydro-Québec announced the launch of a call for proposals to award a block of power containing 300

---

83 A kWh measures the amount of energy consumed or produced over a given period of time, i.e. 1 kWh = 1,000 watts during 1 hour.

84 In the various examples given in this book, we're assuming an exchange rate of 10,000 USD per BTC.

85 https://www.journaldequebec.com/2019/10/04/hydro-quebec-perd-des-ventes-dun-milliard-par-annee

megawatts (MW). Unfortunately, at the time of writing, Hydro-Québec is limiting its offer with a disincentive rate of 15 cents per kWh for projects exceeding 50 kW.[86] It should be noted that this rate will remain in effect until the Régie de l'énergie sets the final rates and their terms of service regarding allocation of electricity to the blockchain industry in a decision expected soon. In November 2022, in light of the significant increase in the anticipated demand for electricity and the tightening energy and capacity balances, Hydro-Québec filed a request with the Régie de l'énergie to suspend the allocation of energy to the blockchain industry.[87]

A SOLUTION TO GAS FLARING

Upstream Data Inc.[88] offers to use gas that would otherwise be flared in the oil and gas industry, with modular equipment installed near the methane gas leaks, thus turning this gas into electricity and then into bitcoins. The recovery of this methane and its combustion, transforming it into electricity, is desirable from an environmental point of view since methane is a more powerful greenhouse gas than CO_2. I invite you to read Stephen Barbour's article on the subject: https://medium.com/@steveg-barbour/there-will-be-bitcoin-d02d486a5d6b

In the Virunga National park in the Democratic Republic of the Congo, deep in the jungle, the park authorities built a few hydroelectric plants to supply electricity to the nearby population. In the wait for the transport infrastructure to be built, the park is currently using the electricity generated by the plants to mine Bitcoin. The monetization of the electricity helps finance the park activities while waiting for the completion of the electricity transport infrastructure.

These are just three examples of using existing energy surpluses or losses to generate bitcoins. El Salvador gave us a fourth example recently: when they got involved in Bitcoin, they started using the geothermal energy generated by their volcanoes to mine bitcoins! As Bitcoin's price rises, we'll see more of these kinds of initiatives come to fruition.

---

86 https://www.hydroquebec.com/blockchain/
87 http://news.hydroquebec.com/en/press-releases/1884/growth-in-electricity-demand-expected-to-continue-in-quebec/
88 https://www.upstreamdata.ca/

THE END OF THE BLOCK SUBSIDY

But what will happen once all the bitcoins have been mined? That's a great question, and there's a very simple answer to it: nothing. Nothing at all. The very last halving event will be no different from every other halving event that will have preceded it, other than for the minor detail that it will put a permanent end to the block subsidy. By the year 2140, miners will only be rewarded with transaction fees for mining new blocks. As the block subsidy continues to dwindle every four years until 2140, the market will gradually adjust itself to the slow and steady pace of these halving events. In February 2010, Satoshi wrote the following regarding this subject on bitcointalk.org:

> *"In a few decades when the reward gets too small, the transaction fee will become the main compensation for nodes."*

EVOLUTION THROUGH SECONDARY LAYERS

In terms of technology, while its core network will probably change very little, Bitcoin will evolve through additional layers or side chains on top of the base layer. The Lightning and Liquid[89] networks are shining examples of this concept. These innovations will allow Bitcoin to scale up to support as many transactions as may be necessary, extend its smart contract capabilities, and increase the level of privacy of its transactions, without altering the base-layer protocol. By the way, it is unlikely that you would use the Bitcoin network to buy a cup of coffee on-chain, as the transaction fees may very well exceed the value of the purchase. It is through secondary layers that Bitcoin will be able to adapt to these kinds of use cases.

The next section of this book offers three bitcoiner interviews as a complement or conclusion to this chapter on Bitcoin's future. As our three protagonists work in the Bitcoin field, they each present a vision of what the future holds from their perspective. This is the best way I could find to conclude this book. I hope they inspire you as much as they inspired me.

---

89 https://liquid.net

INTERVIEWS

Francis Pouliot, CEO of Bull Bitcoin and Bylls

On a sunny afternoon in June, I had the chance to spend a few hours with Francis Pouliot. Although the meeting was conducted via video call, I truly felt like I had spent the afternoon with him over a nice refreshing drink on the balcony of his apartment in Montreal. Francis literally gave me a history lesson on Bitcoin's obscure origins with incomparable passion and enthusiasm.

Francis holds a degree in International Studies from the University of Montreal as well as a Master's degree in Public Policy Analysis from King's College London. Upon graduation, he started working at the Fraser Institute in Montreal where he analyzed public health policy. He then moved to the Montreal Economic Institute where he worked as a public policy analyst. It was during this time that he came into contact with a group of bitcoiners from Quebec City. Francis obtained funding to conduct an analysis of Bitcoin as part of his job as an analyst at the Montreal Economic Institute. He began his research around the time that the Bitcoin Embassy moved into its Montreal office. He spent his days at the Bitcoin Embassy, as part of his research, surrounded by bitcoiners from the early days, to whom he could ask all his questions. After a while, the embassy group offered Francis a job as a public affairs director at the embassy. During this time, Francis accomplished a lot promoting Bitcoin education. He has developed several guides on the subject for the general public. His appearance before the Canadian Senate to make presentations about Bitcoin inspired the introduction of recent legislation governing the operations of virtual currency trading platforms in Canada.[90]

"We realized that the biggest challenge was in education, so we opened the first floor of the embassy to the public."

90 https://twitter.com/francispouliot_/status/1267130517549391873

© Dicoland

The first floor of the embassy building thus became a kind of information booth for Bitcoin. People came in to ask all sorts of questions. Francis and a few embassy volunteers were happy to answer them.

> *"That's why in Montreal there's a sort of 'mega cluster' of bitcoiners. I would say we've had over 20,000 visits."*

In 2015, after introducing thousands of people to Bitcoin through the embassy's information booth, Francis felt that his educational work was behind him. He planned to launch an online Bitcoin exchange service. This decision to build his own service was precipitated by a fortuitous event that took place on the south side of the border. A well-known classified ads site with an adult section saw all of its payment partners leave one after the other. The site was already accepting Bitcoin payments, but overnight, Bitcoin had become the only payment method available to its customers. As it turns out, the embassy under Francis' leadership had already produced a guide detailing the steps to take to transfer bitcoins to this ad service. The site in question, seeking to provide solutions for its users, placed the guide on its home page. An avalanche of calls ensued. The platform's users who wished to publish ads using paid services all found themselves using the guide which contained the embassy's telephone number.

> *"At one point, there were eight of us answering the phone or replying to text messages."*

Aware that there was a real demand for acquiring bitcoins in a simple yet secure way, Francis launched his own company, Satoshi Portal, offering a Bitcoin acquisition service with Bitcoin Outlet, Bull Bitcoin's forerunner. He later acquired bylls.com, a service that allows people to sell bitcoins to pay their bills. Between this acquisition and the rebranding of Bitcoin Outlet to Bull Bitcoin in 2019, Francis focused on the infrastructure and technology behind both companies. In the wake of failed attempts by some groups to take control of Bitcoin's destiny on the protocol level,[91] he and a fellow developer created the backend[92] application Cyphernode. He did not want his services to be dependent upon third parties that chose to

---

91 Francis is referring to the SegWit2x proposal where certain entities in the Bitcoin ecosystem failed in their attempt to impose an increased block size in the Bitcoin blockchain.

92 The software infrastructure behind the operation of a computer system that is not directly accessed by the user, typically responsible for storing and manipulating data.

be on the dark side of Bitcoin's history.

When asked about Bitcoin's most important features, Francis said that he believes Bitcoin's immutability and resistance to censorship are its most prominent attributes.

For Francis, Bitcoin's future will revolve around its primary use case, money, and more specifically as a unit of account. Francis emphasizes that Bitcoin is a direct competitor to fiat currencies, gold, and real estate.

> *"The alternatives to Bitcoin (gold, real estate, payment service providers, the stock market) all have a few things in common: they are all based on the fiat currency system. If fiat currencies collapse, everything collapses."*

Listening again to the recording of the interview, the image that came to mind that best sums up what Francis was saying was a famous line from an American movie: "If you build it, they will come." Francis has spent the better part of the last decade educating the public about Bitcoin, and then preparing a backend application to get the tools ready for hyperbitcoin-ization.[93] I think the classified ads site episode had a significant effect on Francis' vision of what the future holds for Bitcoin. In my opinion, this incident was a kind of wake-up call for him. Francis realized that it was necessary for him, but more importantly for the Bitcoin ecosystem as a whole, to prepare for the next Bitcoin rush.

---

93 Hyperbitcoinization is the point of no return in the democratization and widespread use of Bitcoin after the eventual decline of fiat currencies.

INTERVIEWS

Thibaud Maréchal, Ops & Strategy at zkSNACKs and Contributor for Wasabi Wallet

It was in the middle of Thibaud's vacation that I had a video call with him. I would have much preferred to talk to him on a terrace in the South of France on this beautiful sunny afternoon, but alas, that will wait for another time! Thibaud and I have been working together on a few projects, including the French translation of Yan Pritzker's *Inventing Bitcoin*.

Thibaud left France for Canada after high school. He studied information systems at McGill University. In 2015, he joined a technology investment fund that notably invested in a few Bitcoin companies, including Blockstream. During this tenure, Thibaud participated in the development of a cryptocurrency investment thesis for this fund. One of the problems identified by this research is the challenge of keeping private keys, which is quite complex to manage. Thibaud tells me that the financial manager of the fund in question could not see himself managing millions of dollars in cryptocurrencies on simple hardware wallets, hidden in a drawer. In the process of finding solutions to this problem, Thibaud met with the Knox company, where four engineers looked into the matter. One of the founders of Knox, who had previously worked in insurance, was already working on a method to measure digital risk and develop actuarial models to "import" them from the physical world to the digital world. This aspect is all the more important for fiduciary investors because of their obligation to use insured custodial services. Following this meeting, Thibaud joined the Knox team in 2018.

The first time Thibaud heard about Bitcoin was during a macroeconomics class in 2012 in which the professor depicted an anecdote related to the black market in drugs. The professor had described the dark web and explained that in order to obtain goods there, one had to first obtain a kind of bizarre Internet currency called Bitcoin.

"Coming from a nice and tidy little French family, the first impression it gave me was that Bitcoin was only for the black markets, that it was something illegal."

Thibaud didn't think about Bitcoin at all for at least two years. In 2014, during a student exchange program with Argentina, he attended a university student club whose members played the stock market and traded cryptocurrencies. It was during this time that he completed a thesis on the monetary history of the country. Upon his return, he was once again introduced to Bitcoin when Francis Pouliot of the Bitcoin Embassy was distributing Bitcoin paper wallets on campus.

"Then, I heard about Bitcoin again when Tim Draper bought back the bitcoins that had been seized in the Silk Road[94] collapse, and that's when I started to get more seriously interested in the subject."

Thibaud candidly admits that he jumped into the blockchain and "crypto" world with both feet.

"At first, I was deep into the rhetoric, like—no you see, Bitcoin is old technology, blockchain and crypto are what's going to revolutionize the world. Unfortunately, I had very little understanding of monetary history and economics at that point."

He recounts that it was his meeting with Saifedean Ammous[95] at a conference in Toronto that sealed his fate regarding his involvement in Bitcoin. He realizes that in the end, the only thing worth having is Bitcoin, with the strength of its network. The rest is nothing more than marketing and scams.

When asked about his motivations for changing jobs to join a Bitcoin company, Thibaud recalls having hesitated before taking the leap, adding that the industry has not yet earned its full recognition.

---

94 Silk Road was a black market on the dark web. The website was shut down by the FBI in 2014.

95 Saifedean Ammous is the author of *The Bitcoin Standard.*

"That's the view from the outside though. Now that I'm in it, I only meet incredible, curious, intelligent people. There's a lot of ethics among bitcoiners, there's an enormous amount of integrity."

Another aspect that appealed to Thibaud at the beginning of his involvement in Bitcoin is that anyone curious, hard-working, and who wants to make things better can contribute to Bitcoin, regardless of their status or professional experience.

When asked about the goals he is trying to achieve with his job in the Bitcoin world, Thibaud tells me that his goal is to fight against the loss and theft of bitcoins.

"We would like to make owning bitcoins less of a concern for beginners."

He recently started taking some web development courses with the goal of one day being able to contribute to open-source projects to work on improving user interfaces and user experience.

"Bitcoin is still in its infancy. There's still a lot to be done, especially when it comes to user interface and user experience."

For Thibaud, the most important property of Bitcoin is its scarcity. According to him, this characteristic of Bitcoin has the potential to change the individual who owns it.

"Bitcoin's scarcity changes your relationship with time and money. Bitcoin's scarcity will change the world we live in, because it changes the individual."

Bitcoin has been a real vector of change for him in terms of his social relationships, his diet, and the management of his finances.

"Changes in society don't come from top-down decisions, they emerge from the bottom up through individuals. The fact that the number of bitcoins is strictly limited makes you constantly ask yourself the question, 'Should I really be spending these satoshis?' That simple question has the potential to change your view of life and consumption."

Listening to the interview again, I concluded that, for Thibaud, Bitcoin has the potential to bring about an anthropological revolution first and foremost rather than a technological one. I tend to agree with this premise.

Maciej Cepnik, Canadian and Mexican Ambassador for Bitrefill

At the end of my workday on a Thursday in June, Maciej did me the favor of joining me for a virtual happy hour for an interview. Every time I have the chance to chat with another bitcoiner, it's always the same story: topics are numerous and anecdotes abound. Maciej himself pointed this out to me.

> *"It's always easy to get in touch with a fellow bitcoiner; the connection often happens naturally, it's never forced."*

It's thanks to Maciej and his involvement in Bitcoin Montreal that I had the privilege of getting in touch with several key players who contributed, in their own ways, to the completion of this book. In fact, during our chat (because yes, it was more of a chat than an interview) we realized how easy it is to draw parallels between Bitcoin (the protocol) and its community, both of which are essentially networks. For example, Metcalfe's Law tells us that the utility of a network is proportional to the square of the number of its participants. This is true for Bitcoin, but it's also true for its community. As the number of contacts in this community increases, the value of the network inevitably increases too. The book you are holding in your hands is tangible proof of this.

During the "interview," Maciej tells me how he dropped out of finance school to launch his Bitcoin startup company with his friends and colleagues. Maciej was introduced to Bitcoin quite early in his life. After a few rather unwise (in his own words) investment attempts, a friend introduced him to Bitcoin, and that's when he started to get more serious about it. Maciej and his friends immediately understood Bitcoin's value. They did make a few investments in other cryptocurrencies at first, but they realized even then that Bitcoin's unique features made it the ulti-mate investment in their eyes.

Maciej describes the importance of community in his Bitcoin learning process, almost nostalgically recounting some of the anecdotes from the meetups organized by Francis Pouliot.

> *"Bitcoin is peer-to-peer, the best way to talk about it is face-to-face."*

When asked what motivated him to pursue a career in Bitcoin, Maciej explains that he and his associates have always had the goal of becoming a Canadian (and even a global) educational reference in Bitcoin matters, especially regarding the security and management of Bitcoin assets. Maciej points out that in this field, it's not always easy to stand out from the crowd.

For Maciej, one of Bitcoin's most important characteristics is that it is uncensorable, that no one can stop you from using it as money. He mentions that people go as far as using radio waves to share information on the network, or even satellites to download the blockchain. Scarcity is also one of Bitcoin's most important characteristics in his opinion.

Maciej sees the future of Bitcoin as follows: in the next 10 to 20 years, Bitcoin will be our lifeboat in a storm of financial and monetary uncertainty. In his view, it is the only financial product that is "real" in the sense that you can vouch for its validity and hold it yourself. However, he does not believe in total hyperbitcoinization whereby every country on Earth would adopt Bitcoin as money. He even mentions a scenario in which the US dollar would become deflationary if too many countries wanted to use the US dollar as their currency. In his opinion, Bitcoin could create a new class of influential and powerful people, emerging from a parallel system to gold. For Maciej, it is quite plausible that Bitcoin's total market cap will reach or exceed that of gold. He believes that financial services may develop on top of Bitcoin, much like the current financial system. He does not believe in complete decentralization, suggesting that there will always be a power struggle.

> *"If you want to beat the US dollar, you're going to run into the raw power of those that defend it."*

He concludes that Bitcoin's secret weapon is its insidiousness. Members of government who are aware of Bitcoin could very well affect changes from within.[96]

---

96 And it has well and truly begun. On July 22, 2020, the OCC (Office of the Comptroller of the Currency) in the United States announced that banks will now be able to act as cryptocurrency depositories. What is very interesting here is that the "acting Comptroller of the Currency" of this US federal agency is Brian P. Brooks, former Chief Legal Officer of Coinbase Global Inc. On September 16, 2020, Kraken, a well-known exchange platform, announces that Kraken Financial is recognized by the state of Wyoming as a chartered bank.

Hodl: This word is a variation of the word "hold" which simply means "to hold on to your bitcoins." In other words, not selling your bitcoins under any circumstances. When Bitcoin's price plummets, bitcoiners often call out "Hodl" as a warning not to succumb to the temptation to sell.

Whales: The term "whale" is used to identify investors who hold many bitcoins and with the potential to influence the market.

Lambo: The ultimate symbol of success for some bitcoiners, for whom buying a Lamborghini would be the proof that they made it.

Nocoiner: A term used to refer to people who are outside the cryptocurrency world.

To the moon: This expression is used by bitcoiners to illustrate that Bitcoin's price will figuratively rise to the moon.

In Chapter 6, we described a scenario in which you are purchasing a gift card with the bitcoins your friend gave you as a gift. We mentioned that your wallet could use UTXOs with balances of 0.002 BTC and 0.003 BTC to complete the transaction, as illustrated here:

mtgoRbUoc424NxbLoMamTPYhwS9HBiq5eB - *0.002 BTC*
mxgX9zrwQuyQ6Pz6LyBYDwVzxhdcAh6WZB - *0.003 BTC*

2NA9YcT14V7x7i4UHydH7GgKLU8N9QsXnfw - *0.005 BTC*

However, if you go to the details of the transaction that transferred funds to the following address: *2NA9YcT14V7x7i4UHydH7GgKLU8N9QsXnfw*, you will notice that the wallet decided to combine three transactions like so instead:

mtgoRbUoc424NxbLoMamTPYhwS9HBiq5eB - *0.002 BTC*
2MydCQjg7ftPp6rnBdaGaVJ114cfBba8PQL - *0.0025 BTC*

2MzgHCqTtyPWqHUN8RFx3WRvVJ6eD2DW1LD - *0.0075 BTC*

2NA9YcT14V7x7i4UHydH7GgKLU8N9QsXnfw - *0.005 BTC*

2MxxmbHMzGTcKAZUTbHX9UE2DA2uXb6uSrA - *0.007 BTC*

CHANGE ADDRESSES

This example allows us to introduce the concept of a change address. When the balance of the UTXO(s) in a transaction is not used in its entirety, a change address is automatically generated by the wallet to accommodate the return of this money. In the example above, 0.007 BTC are returned to a new change address of the wallet that initiated the transaction. This is exactly the same principle as if you buy a $3 product with a $10 bill and get $7 back.

DUST

Two factors could potentially explain the choice of these three transactions made by the wallet. The first is transaction fees. The second is the wallet's desire to minimize "dust." Dust is simply UTXOs containing a few dozens or hundreds of satoshis that would cost more to send in transaction fees than their underlying value. Kind of like mailing an envelope containing a nickel while using a stamp that's worth a dollar. To prevent this, the wallet adds another UTXO to the transaction, in this case 2MzgHCqTtyPWqHUN8RFx3WRvVJ6eD2DW1LD - 0.0075 BTC to prevent only "dust" being sent to the change address. By adding this UTXO, the wallet combines the "change" to be returned from each of the UTXOs and sends it to a new change address.

TRANSACTION FEES

In the early days of the Bitcoin network, there was no need to pay transaction fees. As the volume of transactions increased and blocks began to fill up, paying a transaction fee ensured that your transaction would be chosen by the miners so that it could be included in the next block. In the transaction examples above, we did not mention transaction fees for simplicity's sake. In summary, the reason why a UTXO of 0.002 BTC and a UTXO of 0.003 BTC are not enough to send 0.005 BTC is because you need to add a transaction fee.

VERIFYING A DOWNLOAD SIGNATURE

In Chapters 6 and 7, we described how to install some of the software in the Bitcoin ecosystem. One of the dangers in downloading software from the Internet is obviously the risk of downloading malware. This risk exists for all software that we install on our devices, but it is mitigated today by the availability of various "app store" type platforms, in which a third party (Apple, Microsoft, Google) provides a minimal amount of control over the applications that are there. However, when you download an application directly from a website, you have to trust the website in question. As if that was not enough, there is also the risk that the file will be intercepted or that it ends up being different from the file initially offered by the site in question. This risk is even more worrisome when it comes to Bitcoin-related apps. An app could simply ask you to enter your private key and steal your bitcoins. A malicious app could also function exactly like a wallet and wait for you to add a few coins into your wallet before confiscating them, like a sword of Damocles hanging over your head, ready to ruin your life at any moment. Installing a compromised version of Bitcoin software could turn your Bitcoin trial into a disastrous experience in one fell swoop.

Fortunately, there are procedures to verify the authenticity of the code contained in the files that you download. There is a relatively simple way to check whether or not the file provided by the developer responsible for an app is indeed the same file you downloaded, removing any doubt that a malicious person may have intercepted the file to modify it. In fact, it is possible for the developer to sign the software installation file and publish his public key on his website, or better yet, present it at a developer conference. You can then use this public key to verify that the file that you just downloaded has indeed been signed by the private key of the developer in question

myUUXn6LfAm6MN8ae1xkVkthNSjFShQKWd

mjPrzFr84SRXPTygRGTiWJkQ8SZwNdSd93

mxgX9zrwQuyQ6Pz6LyBYDwVzxhdcAh6WZB

mtgoRbUoc424NxbLoMamTPYhwS9HBiq5eB

mw9qzMLnGiiuiXZJy3tGYnDbMzqavuWoHs

mqe6pbyhaYVa1jkKGYBJfG7Hhm9CqMqpHd

2NA9YcT14V7x7i4UHydH7GgKLU8N9QsXnfw

ACKNOWLEDGEMENTS

Thanks to Valérie and David for giving me the idea to write this book. Thanks to my friends and colleagues for putting up with my tirades about Bitcoin. Thanks to Alec for introducing me to cryptocurrency mining. Thanks to Nick for answering my hundred thousand questions in my early days. Thanks to my family for their support during all these months of research and writing. Thank you to my editor, Marie, for helping me put my ideas into words. Thanks to Francis, Maciej and Thibaud for letting themselves be interviewed.

Thanks to all the bitcoiners on "Bitcoin Twitter" for all their insights: especially @saifedean @pierre_rochard @francispouliot_ @thibm_ @CepnikMaciej @stephanlivera @edstromandrew @jimmysong @thebitcoinrabbi.

Thanks to the respective authors of all the works cited in this book. Thanks to Bitcoin Montréal for the great meetings and their contents. Thanks to the *Formation Continue* department at Maisonneuve College for daring to offer my Bitcoin course to the public, which laid the groundwork for this book. Thanks to Maxime for the illustrations and the cover. Thanks to Audrey for proofreading and advice. Thanks to Jonathan Herscovici for all the tips surrounding the French reality of cryptocurrency. Thanks to the Office québécois de la langue française for its work on cryptocurrency vocabulary, which helped me write the French edition of this book. Thanks to Jonathan who helped me kickstart this translation. Thank you to Henry J.K.I. Young who completed the bulk of the translation and went above and beyond to make the book better!

Made in the USA
Monee, IL
14 April 2023

31882467R00083